Presented to the
University of Michigan
by The Author
June 24, 1862

TRACTS FOR TO-DAY.

BY

M. D. CONWAY,

MINISTER OF THE FIRST CONGREGATIONAL CHURCH, CINCINNATI, OHIO.

CINCINNATI:
TRUMAN & SPOFFORD.
1858.

TO MY PARENTS

I dedicate this book;—knowing that, whatever they shall find here which shall recall painful differences of belief, it would grieve them far more to think that I had swerved from the lessons of directness and sincerity which, by word and life, they have ever taught as before all, and which they have a right to claim from me always and everywhere.

LETTER

To a Minister of the Baltimore (Methodist) Conference.

DEAR FRIEND—

Your letter is one of the many of a similar kind, received not only from members of our dear old Conference, but from those who were class-mates at Carlisle, members of my circuits, or friends of myself and relatives in Virginia. "Why I have left my old associations and communion," were indeed a question requiring a long answer. But since it is asked by all my friends (and they have every right to ask it), I have been thinking how I could follow out your suggestion and publish an answer. I have concluded to put forth a small collection of discourses, such as have occurred in my regular ministrations. For it is in these that a preacher's heart and life get best garnered after all. I am not of that school who have one set of thoughts for the study, another for the pulpit: I can only preach what is the last result of my own mind. Therefore, though I could wish that the urgency of a city parish allowed more time for completeness and elegance, these thoughts are my real self, and as such are, to me, sacred. From such statements it is easy to trace the threads running back to all I have left,—for an apple preserves the mark of the blossom which bore it. M. D. C.

CINCINNATI, *January*, 1858.

CONTENTS.

THE DIVINE WORKER.

WIST ye not that I must be about my Father's business?
It is finished!

IT has seemed to me that these two passages of the New Testament, combining the earliest and last words of Christ during his earthly ministry, belong to each other. When we remember that, in his childhood, the idea of a purpose in life arose before him, and a clear light from his soul revealed an object crying out for accomplishment, whose cries he alone could hear and aid, we are thrilled with the first words which fell from his lips, when his parents found him, a boy of twelve, sitting with the doctors—*I must be about my Father's work!* And as we read of his steadfast adhesion to that work, following on through fire and thorns and the dark valley, it becomes the triumphant password of the eternal gates when he cried, *It is finished!* And he bowed his head and gave up the ghost.

Thou beautiful, wonderful child! thy words bring us directly to the core of all vitality, strength and excellence! We come to the idea of a personal existence slowly, to the faith that God has sent us into the world, as individuals, because each one had separately something to do there, which no created being had done or could do for us, and with reference to which work every atom and fiber of our nature was prepared. But Christ, in his boyhood and that of the world, has already prepared his heart's altar and sacrifice, and the flame rises smokeless and pure! My friends, any one who has been spending strength, baffling the waves of sense, to reach the strong shore of the spirit, will need no miracle beyond this to attest the divine illumination of our Messiah.

And thus, from whatsoever side we approach it, we find Christ's character more and more divine, because more and more human; for the deep heart within us all announces, Thus must it be with each man who is worthy the room he occupies in the world, that he should be about his Father's work, and that his last consciousness should be that, according to the best strength given, *It is finished!*

There can be nothing now so needed among men as the recognition of a personal calling. The arguments which prove the truth of this Individualism are the simplest; they are drawn from the most trusted articles of every man's creed: and yet it is *so* simple as to be ignored, that this is at last the cure which poor wounded Humanity needs, and with many dumb signs has long been seeking to make known, *that each man should come out in terrible energy of thought, word, and act, with whatever wells up natively within him.*

I have said that it is drawn from the most trusted articles of every man's creed,—for no one will say that things are given over to chance or Satan; that Human beings, with their endless possibilities, higher and lower, are the mere spawn of the Universe; sent here with little if any forethought or afterthought, or often, as Malthus taught, sent here to great disadvantage in the light of political economy. But every one's first teaching to his child is to say, when asked, "Who made you?" "God." Why should it not strike into his heart then to say, What is this? The Eternal God made thee! Then, O child, if he made thee, he meant thee!

This let us rest on for Eternity, that God does nothing by redundance; that there is nothing so small, not a dust-atom, but serves its part toward balancing the Universe of Stars; that the Ineffable glory goes as surely into a butterfly's as into an angel's wing. And all the grandeur of the outward Universe cannot be so mysterious and momentous as a man. Oh, friends! there is another Universe into which a man must be born besides this without: it is that which hath its infinite growths and splendors within his soul,—where great and holy thoughts and affections arise and shine, until the nightly host of Heaven grows dim.

Thus "know thyself," "live thyself," "be true to thyself," sum up for each the essence of Decalogue, Prophets and Testaments; and man only becomes man, when he retires to the holy oracle within, and asks,

"Lord, what wouldst thou have ME to do?" and then abandons himself to that work, however strange, or difficult or meanly associated such work may be.

I confess now that I do not believe those who say that the mass of mankind do and can have no such experience of a personal relation to God and his Universe. I do not wish a better proof that they may and do have it than the conviction of entire adequacy to his calling in life, which every man feels, and his indifference to adequacy in the business of others. Men are not sensitive outside of their own circles of duties, but are very much so within them. You may easily persuade a physician that he cannot preach a sermon or a minister that he cannot prescribe for disease; but you shall find it a far more delicate task to assure the physician that he cannot prescribe properly for disease, or the minister that he cannot preach. And so of every sphere of labor or profession; the blacksmith does not care to be thought a good carpenter, nor the carpenter a lawyer—but each would be filled with mortification or anger at a proof or charge of inability in respect of that which he follows as a calling. And this is not conceit, nor any low, but a very high, instinct. It is the witness that each one has within him of a divine right to excel in that to which he has been drawn, and which he knows is the only one thing wherein he *can* excel. He feels that he has a claim on all things and all men to help him toward perfection, so long as he faithfully works the work of Him who sent him, and who infolds the work proper for him in the soul of every man he sends; which inevitably reveals itself, at the proper time, hand in hand with the measure of strength needed. He feels that none can gainsay his sufficiency for his task, except through his faithlessness or their enmity. So well may one be sensitive to criticism.

It is very sad to see that this faith in the divine authority of the division of labor has long been a Church abstraction. They tell us, God surely ordains in his Church, or among his people, (the phrases are various,) that one man should be a layman, another a deacon, another a priest or a rector, another a bishop—so it is expressed and illustrated by Paul's figure of the body and members. But when we would declare that God is King of *all* the Earth, and not of their self-styled Church or people of God alone; and affirm that He makes the true poets, composers, mechanics, and earnest-workers of all kinds, and ordains them to their offices a great deal more than their churchmen and dignitaries—why a dimness comes over their eyes to such a degree that they declare *you* to be wandering in the dark. And this unbelief is assisted by the consciousness of too many who have to say: I am not what I am by a divine impulse, but by the ordination of kind friends and circumstances. They therefore declare, that no one has any authoritative mission to any special office. And these, my friends, are dead, and must be left in sorrow to bury their dead.

A nobler doctrine is taught us by the unerring experience of the great throbbing heart of Mankind itself, as recorded by the one infallible historian Human Language. The word which has been adopted to express that by which a man lives, is CALLING. It would seem that by a common understanding, which a universally understood word always expresses, that which a man does is not what he has selected, but which has selected or called him. The word would imply that a voice has been heard and obeyed.

And it is because the common heart is thus so far in advance of the Church, because the Church needs, more than those to whom it preaches, conversion to God, to a faith that not one man nor hair of his head, nor emotion or power in him is forgotten before Him, and that this is equally true of John Smith, the cobbler, and Paul, the apostle,—it is because of this, I say, that the chief encounter of an upstriving individual manhood in any one is with the Church. The first question which brother dissenters ask each other on meeting is, *How did you get on with the Church, when you acted thus or avowed such opinions?* That being told, the whole story is told. No great art is there which has not been placed under ban of the Church. The man who introduced something quicker than a minim into music came near paying for it with his life, and not until they became too popular for the temptation to be resisted did the Church encourage the painting and sculpture which pietistic impurity, even to this day, often pronounces immoral because true. There never was one of the Holy Order of scientific men who escaped the censure of the Church, if he was brave and free; and the progress of ages makes very little difference,—Agassiz finds it about as hard as Galileo.

One instance I have heard, where a religious body allowed God's blood to circulate freely through its veins; and it is so remarkable that I will relate it. There was in a country-town of Pennsylvania a boy who gave early indication of a genius and passion for painting. He was the child of Quaker parents. The chief—I had nearly written *only*—error of this society, is an ascetic intolerance of whatever contributes simply to the sense of beauty, not seeing that Beauty in and for itself must be good, because God made it and gave it the key of the human heart. The Quaker parents of little Benjamin sought, therefore, to repress this inclination for painting which had so often been rebuked by their leaders. But to repress it was not easy: the God raged within him like a fever, and inspired a scorn of other work. The affectionate parents went around and conversed with many members of the society on the subject; and, after repeated discussions, it was resolved to lay the matter before the Lord, since the Lord had made the boy. So they gathered together in their old meeting-house where, doubtless, many a testimony had been given to the vanity of the fine arts, and there sat in holy silence awaiting a message from the good Father as to what should be done with the pertinacious little Benjamin. And when the voice, which never fails to be heard when other voices are silent, came; and one declared that there was a mistake somewhere, and that either their antagonism to painting was an impiety, or else God had erred in sending that young soul into the world with such inevitable tendencies, and furthermore suggested that the blunder might be on their part, they all received his words just as if they had come from the Bible. As his parents were very poor, they all contributed something to have him educated in his art. The fruitful years grew on, and little Benjamin had reached the highest position as an artist in the most cultivated of all countries; and he sent across the sea a great painting to his State, by the exhibition and value of which thousands of poor mutes of the institution which he endowed have learned to bless the name of Benjamin West, who sent them "Christ healing the sick."

When before did a religious organization ever ordain one to the service of the true life within him; to the service of immortal beauty;—and thus, taking him by the hand, bid him God-speed in accomplishing his Father's business? Yet many a so-called heathen has taught the Church this mission. "The first time (cries the ancient Persian Prophet) that I was called to the world above, the heavens and stars said unto me, O Sasan! we have bound up our loins in the service of Yezdan, and never withdrawn from it, because he is worthy of praise; and we are filled with astonishment how mankind can wander so far from the commands of God."

It is indeed the way of health,—to mind one's own business. For no man can have any business unless God give it him; every occupation possible having some relation to the necessities of our mind, body, or soul—which of course are of him. In faithful attention to our own affair, we place ourselves in harmony with nature and the music of the spheres, which though ruled by one law follow each its own orbit. Many divine currents of life seem to flow out to invigorate us when we fall into our spheres of duty. But to him who attempts to heed the world, or fashion, or self-interest, and attach himself to any work to which he is not called by temperament or craving, the Heavens shall be unyielding as brass, and no fast-flowing gush of inspiration shall ever come, like the sirocco of the desert, to lift up his poor dust to stand in solid pillars against the Heavens.

Happy is he whose heart is in his hand! What his hand findeth to do he shall do with a consciousness of might which may, with better reason than Napoleon had, regard it as a proof of the weakness of the human mind to suppose it can be resisted. All things willingly fly to be his servants. By a noble army of such, spreading through all time, comes the proverb, clear as a sunbeam to every such one now, *Love's labor's light.* Most surely do we feel, when we are fulfilling that which is in the highest sense our *calling*, that not one effort can fail to advance it; that not one instance of opposition from others can fail to advance it; that it goes on in sleeping or waking. No toil for that end is hard. As children dance and dream not of weariness; as the young Mozart pores over his scores, and is only sad when interrupted; as the mother wears away at her sick child's bedside, and will only complain if any one takes her place; as birds sing, and waters fall, and flowers yield fragrance,—so easily does any one who finds his true work accomplish it.

This is so certain a rule that we may affirm that after all, the best measure and indication of virtue is success. The Universe is on his side—nature with its laws, the real hearts of all men, the *All*,—from the mote in the sunlight up to the Lord of Hosts, throb and move in sympathy with him. "In all the vocabulary of youth there is no such word as fail," said the old Cardinal Richelieu, to the young man who announced his failure. And work with love is perpetual youth.

But let us not be deceived by the contemptible, vulgar estimates of the street, as to what constitutes success or failure. A splendid estate, money counted to the billion, a white house or a throne—these do not constitute success in life; these may be the miserablest failures. For these, may have been lost incorruptible treasures, gold coined of the pavement of Heaven; a throne pure and high on God's right-hand, whence selfishness, ambition, and injustice have been controlled, may have been paid for this presidency or kingly honor. We often read on marble fronts, *success*, where angels read sadly, *failure*. Nor do poverty, nor pain, nor fetters, nor death by violence or law constitute a failure in life. See up there on the cross him who first fully entered into his Father's work. How they mock him, and cry "Hail king of the Jews! He *said* he was a king. He said he could save others, and cannot save himself!" Why, these men manifestly look upon his claims and life as a complete failure. His life cut off before its greatest vigor; dying by the most ignominious instrument by which one could die—they counted Christianity a failure! Even the disciples seem to have thought so, and fled.

But in that divine heart whose last life-streams were gushing, how far different were the revelations which now we see were true. That day, when all thought Christianity and Jesus a failure, was his coronation day: that cross was his throne, whence he shall ever rule the world; in that darkest moment the true birth-pang of the Universe was past—and before man arose the prospect of a newborn world! Lo, the World's most majestic success!

Let the world have a care that it does not call the most magnificent successes, failures; the worst failures, brilliant successes. But thou, Oh, brother! know that the soul alone is conscious of its full success; and, whether men censure or blame, *knows* that it has achieved all, when the deep heart can bravely take the last words of Christ, and say of its true mission, *It is finished!* And this can alone ever be really felt or said of that thing given you, *that one thing* whereto all your faculties call you: for man has well been compared to the Labrador Spar, which, turned to a sunbeam in various ways is opaque, but when the point of crystallization is turned to the ray, instantly all the colors of the rainbow flash through.

Success comes by this *faith in what we can do*, which is the parent of that wonder-worker, manly enthusiasm. When men feel how real and deep a thing it is to live, and feel that they must be about their father's business, they are moved with the soul's passion: then follows heroic action. Their duty, lying there before them, is then as the breath of their nostrils, and the word comes to them as in ancient days to one chosen to work for Jehovah, "Not by might, nor by power, but by my spirit, saith the Lord of Hosts. Who art thou, O, great mountain! before Zerubbabel thou shalt become a plain!"

Oh, how much of the mediocrity if not meanness of our lives, how much of our tragical failure, is to be attributed to a lack of enthusiasm! Three words of advice, I remember, John Wesley had for a young man: *Be in earnest.* What we want first is earnestness, and what we want last is earnestness—that hearty enthusiasm which can come only where a man feels conscious that he is in the right, and which carries him like lightning to his point. Men call it bad names, I know, call it fanaticism, ignorance, wildness, ambition, imprudence. They praise much the virtues of calmness and self-possession. But as we look back now we see, that the brightest jewels on the brow of history are the names of those who obeyed some high impulse, and gave all to it. Men said of them, that they were carrying things too far; they said this of Luther and all the Reformers. And many suffered themselves to be led by a reaction from the point to which these had gone. *We see* that an instinct in them, unerring as that which in the bee and silkworm puts human skill to shame, led these men to the *extent* of their work; not a hair's breadth the other side of it—not a hair's breadth this side of it. And we discern some method in the madness of Cromwell's saying, "That a man never rises so high as when he knows not whither he is going."

The one great curse is indifference. It is nothing in itself—for neither you nor I can harm the Universe, nor do any wrong beyond God's power of righting—but only as it indicates how many lives are barren, cold and dead, because they are not drawn by any strong fervor to any one sphere, having long ago denied their Lord of Life, saying, *I know no such duty*. Oh! cannot apathy itself be used as a spur to carry you beyond apathy, which is death.

Young man! Let us be in earnest though Chaos should return! If thou must needs be so, be whimsical, rash, imprudent, mad—so thou be saved from the body of death, which is a hateful indifference to that which through thee would strive to bud and bloom and contribute its quality to all!

If calmness, prudence, sanity are to be made the bushel to hide our little ray, so much the worse for them. But it is not so. Calmness is akin to enthusiasm. What can be more serene than the sunlight which yet incessantly carries on its siege of subtle heats, which presently turn snow and ice into violets and hyacinths? And as men look forth on the world of Humanity, and remembering the burdens of old prophets who sang of the latter-day glory, and the saying concerning Christ, that he "saw the travail of his soul and was satisfied," so fair and perfect even to that exacting eye was the vision of a redeemed world—yet see it frozen by a dread winter; see man's hand lifted against man in war; see trade polluted by dishonesty, so that what we eat and wear is poisoned or stained with crime; see oppression of man by man, until we scarce know in their degradation those own brothers of Christ's—to whom *we* are anything *but* brothers—save by the cry which the eternal spirit within them, though feebler and feebler, still sends to heaven; oh! as we remember this, see this, your worldly doctrine of calmness changes us to marble! Talk to the mother of calmness as her child disappears beneath the wave; then come and talk of it to the soul which sees God's idea, as he *feels* it, and others *see* it trampled under foot of *men*—our leaders standing without, warming themselves by the fire!

There is much need of faith in being about and accomplishing our Father's work. Often our eyes may see that a thing, if done, would be attended with trouble, confusion and danger, while yet the inner voice is clear: *Let it be done—it is right!* Then must we walk and act by faith, not by sight; be true to the inner light, and leave the rest to God, beyond whose control no atom can go. For what is confusion to our poor sight, is Eternal Beauty to God. And even to us, when we can release ourselves from the usual bondage to fear, there is the gleam of a higher good, such as animated Phocion, when in a moment of great temptation of his nation to an injustice, he cried, *Let justice be done though the heavens fall!* I have observed that every *discord* in music in one of its notes suggests and leads into the next chord.

Thus, brothers, let us evolve our idea; let us carve from the hard rude block given each, the God that labors within us to be born. None dream of the pure joy of life who do not obey their hearts. The true and great have always felt this. The last lines written by Britain's first poet, Chaucer, were

Truth to thine own heart
Thy soul shall save.

And it is not the truth and rule of his own work, but of all,—the saying of Sir Philip Sidney, "*Look into thy heart and write.*" Let then no discord or danger appal you. Let the burning thought leap forth in thought, word, act; though the Earth be removed and the Heavens shudder, they shall all at last repeat it forever. To hear this let us wait if need be a million years,—heeding the word which bids us *having done all, to stand!*

Friends enough there will be, warm with love and sincerity, to bid you substitute for this entrance into the sanctuary of the soul, the words of those who have entered it in past times and returned with the messages of the Holy Ghost abiding there. I know how hard it is for man to come face to face with his own deep soul; and how the edge of the Spirit's sword seems less keen when we get it at one or more removes—through Isaiah or Paul. But say to these, O man, No! Thankful am I for the Holy Book, but I also exist now as Paul then; the planets move yet; life yet fills the world; oxygen and hydrogen go to make water, and oxygen and nitrogen, air, now as then; the sun shines, the grass grows to-day; God is as great as ever: dear friends, by the grace of God I also am that I am!

Never was that book written which can come so close as your own soul. Oh the soul—the soul, where man mingles so mysteriously with Infinite Being! Oh vast spirit of man, what heaven so high or hell so deep that thou hast not the key of it! Oh infinite aspirations and endeavors,—clamorous they rise up:

We have strong pinions. We will bear thee, Oh soul, beyond a myriad worlds; the suns shall light us on our way; the planets shall but rest us, each for a day; on —on to the supersolar blaze streaming from the great white throne itself!

I know that this living from within—always from within—is hard; and I would not accuse those many persons who have sold their true and high birthright; for there are ever great interests to offer great prices: but yet must we bear witness to the immutability of spiritual laws. It would not be love to a child which wished to lean too far out of a window, that the law of gravitation which it might violate should be kept secret for the sake of its ignorant inclination. Neither will it be love to any one to ignore the law, that death of soul sits ready to spring on one who goes outside of the law written on that soul; that any compromise or suppression of it for peace or comfort or custom is the tragedy over which the angels weep. For God has not bound the solar systems by a chain of laws and appointed their paths for the heavenly host, and left lawless the souls of men—the only vagrants of the Universe. But he has engraven their paths and laws on these also,—on the "tablets of the heart." In living by these is health and immortal youth and strength; away from them every breath is deadly. Every act of untruthfulness to yourselves is rebellion against God. Every adherence to what is popular, involving rejection of secretly-felt truth, is a repetition of the old cry, "Crucify him! Crucify him! Give us Barabbas, the thief, instead."

> Like as a star,
> That maketh not haste,
> That taketh not rest,
> Let each be fulfilling
> His God-given hest.

Is this not then the true lesson to be derived from the first and last words of Jesus? They fall on us with many touching associations. They bring us to the most solemn of all scenes to the Christian,—the Crucifixion. Up there on the cross is the greatest lover of man. He seems as he is passing from earth to forget all without; to forget the wild mob, the cruel spear, the nails, the crown of thorns. Doubtless his mind centers on this: Have I accomplished his work? His mind reverts to the day when, a child twelve years old, he went down to Jerusalem with his parents, and the idea of his mission dawned on him, as he said: *I must be about my Father's work!* And on from that he traced his life—his toils, his teaching, his griefs. Had he ever been untrue to his soul? Had fear ever induced him to sanction the sins and the superstition of the people, whom he was sent to reform? Oh how sweet and clear was the response in that dear soul: 'No! thou hast overcome; there was no failure; it is fulfilled.' And so he cried "It is finished!" And he bowed his head and died. Hark! Hearest not his voice saying, So live that it may be said of thy work also, IT IS FINISHED!

THE SKEPTIC.

PHILIP findeth Nathaniel and saith unto him: "We have found him of whom Moses in the Law and the Prophets did write—Jesus of Nazareth the son of Joseph." And Nathaniel said unto him, "Can there any good thing come out of Nazareth?" Philip saith unto him, "Come and see." * * * * Jesus saw Nathaniel coming to him, and saith of him, "Behold an Israelite indeed, in whom there is no guile."

THERE is one class of persons in the World who have never had justice done them. I mean the Skeptics. When a person is spoken of as a skeptic, you can see a thrill pass over those present, as if they dreampt of a serpent; and a mournful silence follows every earnest avowal of doubt. And yet it would seem, on investigation, that we have no positive reason for the traditional idea that causes this shudder. Each one of us doubts many times a day; and it is by continually testing things by doubts that we come to correct conclusions in practical affairs. But where the same test is carried into the high matters of the Soul, where it would seem we should be most careful to carry it, we give up the well-tried rule; and when a person is so scrupulous as to entitle him to the name of *skeptic*, we are shocked. Yet it is a state of mind that is usually involved in temperament, and may be traced in the blood to your descent from skeptical or credulous races and families. "The shapings of our heavens," says Charles Lamb, "are the modifications of our constitutions, and Mr. Greatheart or Mr. Feeblemind is born in every one of us."

We see the differences every day. One man will weep in secret that he cannot believe the Incarnation or the miracles; another will swallow all mysteries, and only regret he hasn't more. One poor saint will grope through the world melancholy, doubting if he is regenerate, or if he pleases God; another is perfectly assured that he is of the elect, that he is God's darling, and gives himself no more trouble about it.

Which of these is learning the lesson of this Universe best? Which is the truly humble and surrendered soul? Let that be answered by our first deeper glance at the circumstances of this our mysterious life, where we find ourselves as in mid-ocean, with neither shore in sight—for who can more than dream of the source of the spirit before it entered his body, or of the land whither we are borne by each moment, as by a wave?

The motto of the wise old Gascon, Montaigne, was, *Que sçais-je?* What know I for certain? Modern Philosophy, inquiring into every sphere of science, finds that the uncertainty of our knowledge is the pressing question. While man is but a bundle of senses, he never doubts; Reason is then in its lowest state. But he is presently weaned, as it were, from Nature. And the first separation is the discovery that the senses are at fault in some instances, and therefore are not infallible. The child at play, putting a stick in the water, is astonished to see it broken at the point where it touches the water; but still more amazed is he to find, on taking it out, that it is unbroken. His senses have deceived him. This is his first lesson in the Law of the Refraction of Light. The Man, a child of larger growth, sees that the Earth is flat; and, when he calls in the mountain, hears that some one answers; but presently is astonished to find that he sees a small mast at sea before he sees the hull; and on searching for the sound that answered his call, discovers no one. Here are the first intimations of Perspective, and of the Laws of Acoustics, which explain the Echo as no longer an invisible nymph. You see that *real* knowledge begins by bringing the senses into doubt. Its progress is by a perpetual engendering of doubts, by which one experimenter is led to test the conclusion of the one who preceded him, and perhaps find his position untrue.

What is certain? In natural science, men of equal genius have theories of the stratification of the earth, the earliest appearance of man, etc., which neutralize each other. Historians are just as much at variance. Cæsar's Wars are questioned as being much more insignificant than was supposed, and much reduced in number. Homer is no more the conceded author of the Iliad; and it requires hundreds of learned volumes to show that Orpheus ever existed.

If there was anything we might have fixed on as certain, it might have been once the existence of matter and our own persons. But we are now in the midst of a most heated controversy on this very subject. Lord Brougham has said, "He who has never doubted that he existed, may be sure that he has no aptness for metaphysical inquiries." Whether our senses are to be believed, and whether we should give more certainty or solidity to their objects, than we do to the dreams we have—of which we are equally certain while dreaming? And dreams are not wilder than many things that men testify to having seen: men raised to life, ascending to heaven; health produced by touching the bones of saints; cities let down from the heavens. Pious, unquestionable men have united in scores to testify these things. We are familiar with the sincerest testimonies to miracles the most astounding in our own day, by persons who have no more interest to deceive than the evangelists. How far shall we believe men? What shall we believe? Our own senses?—they deceive us often; if you believe them, you would think two stars close together, which were millions of miles apart. Our own Reason? All of us have given up something we once thought reasonable—why so infallible now?

Who then is the skeptic but he who holds the balances with unflinching, though human hand; who believes that much may be said on all sides, and will not be rash or partial in allowing one to be heard to exclusion of the rest? He is indeed the true ideal man. The finest elements of Nature, the clearest of flame, the finest clay, the lightest air, seem to combine in his composition. As was declared of one in the old Bible, he is as the eyes of the Lord, which run throughout the whole earth. He sees many sides of things where men generally say, "Sit down, eat, and ask no questions." He is the man who comes into the world to consider, σκεπτειν. For the word skeptic, however much we shudder at it, really means the lofty character I have indicated. The Greek word from which it is derived is σκεπτομαι, literally, *I shade my eyes to look steadily at something.* And a skeptic is one who would shade his eyes of all but the light necessary for seeing—would divest himself of all self-interest—would dismiss passion, and steadily examine all that comes to demand his acquiescence. These are the men in all time, who, by earnestly pressing established positions, detect their fallacies, if they have them, make them more certain, if they have them not. The laws of Gravity, Circulation of the Blood, Fluxions, Motions of the Earth, came by skeptics. And those who are not skeptics, have been those who in every age of the world have abused, scourged, burned, crucified those who, by finding these new laws, brought the old order into doubt on which they had fastened themselves as parasites.

But men ask, Are we not warned against Doubt in the Scriptures? Did not Christ, as he reached forward his hand to sinking Peter, cry, "O thou of little faith, wherefore didst thou doubt?" Did he not tell them that if they should have faith and doubt not, they should remove mountains? And there is a phrase coined up by translators and Churches as a sort of bullet for skeptics, taken from Paul, as is said, "Whoso doubteth is damned." But with regard to the few phrases where Christ is said to have rebuked doubt, it is to be observed that the word does not refer to doubt as we mean it, but *hesitation to do what you are already certain of as right.* The word used is ἐδίστασας, and means that kind of doubt which all will unite in reproving; that which stands still before known duty. But Paul says, *Whoso doubteth is damned—if he eat.* (The word does not mean *damned*, but *is judged*). The amount of this and the whole of *Rom.* 14, is this: in regard to the question asked him, whether Christians could eat anything without respect to Jewish prohibitions on certain kinds of flesh, he says: Eat what you will. But if you find eating certain things incites weaker brothers to real excesses, you had best abstain. But if you *doubt* whether you may not be doing wrong, you commit a sin,—for doing anything you are not sure is innocent. It is the same as Cicero's maxim, What a man doubteth to do, that he should shun. On the contrary, it was Paul who called Festus "most noble," in the very moment in which he had declared that he doubted on all those things of which he heard Paul preach!

And I wish now to call to your attention *Christ's treatment of a skeptic.* For the little we know of Nathaniel, which is that I have read you in the text, indicates him as a skeptic. And there is something in this brief history, and especially Christ's singular and earnest commendation of him, which excites a desire to know all we can of him.

Those among the Jews who were really religious, as the studious and wise in all nations, were in the habit of going alone to think and read. The hypocritical loved, as we find elsewhere, to pray, standing in the synagogues and street-corners. It is thus a matter of interest that Nathaniel was found by Philip under a fig-tree, a kind which abounded a short distance from the city. It was there that an eye rested on him that he knew not of; one that could never see this retired meditation without deep interest. It was the eye of Jesus. He also had gone from the busy haunts of men, and doubtless had seen him, when his own spirit was burdened with a world's Evangel, and he would fain commune alone with his Father. So when Jesus was asked by Nathaniel "Whence knowest thou me?" he said, "When thou wast yet under the fig-tree, before Philip called thee, I saw thee." * * There is something here left to the imagination to supply. For the bare fact of Christ's having seen him under the fig-tree can scarcely account for the great emotion with which he instantly exclaimed, *Rabbi, thou art the son of God, the King of Israel.* Some have thought that this arose from Christ's having supernaturally seen him under the tree; and the disciples may have so understood it. But, though I shall not oppose those who find this to be the best element discoverable here, I will only say that I think otherwise. I believe that there was something known to Jesus and Nathaniel alone, relative to his being in that seclusion. Men do not ordinarily leave the city for solitude and thought. Some earnest emotion there was which led this soul away from the shallowness of the city and the hypocrisy of the Temple,—some knowledge of the Father which seeth in secret it implied, which at once riveted the attention of Jesus. We know not what earnest prayer that the Messiah might come to redeem the people went from Nathaniel's heart. We know not what immortal tears were wept in that retreat over the woes and sins of his nation and himself. But we do know, that it was in the mind of Jesus to compare this favorably with the apathy and evil which he everywhere saw: *here*, at least, was no hollow pretense, but real fervor and feeling. And now as he was selecting his disciples, he probably sent Philip to the place where he had seen this good man. For the record says, Philip *findeth* Nathaniel, as if he had been seeking him. And when he saw Nathaniel coming he said, *Behold an Israelite indeed in whom is no guile.* As if he should have said: "There are in the city thousands of Israelites by circumcision; children of Abraham by the mint-tithe and common process. Here is one *indeed;* not outwardly so much as they who are in the Temple,—but, in reality, because within him is none of their hypocrisy or guile.'

And yet, this man of such earnestness and beautiful simplicity, who was declared by Christ without guile, *was a skeptic.* When Philip found him under the tree he cried with entire confidence,—"We have found him, of whom Moses in the Law, and the Prophets, did write,—Jesus of Nazareth, Joseph's Son." But he finds no ready belief. The incredulous answer is, "*Can any good come out of Nazareth?*" That city had become proverbial for the degradation and sinfulness of its inhabitants; and Nathaniel had all the reason to doubt which we should have if told that the Christ had come a second time at Paris or Rome. We must wait to see much evidence first: for we have known from them much evil and little good.

Though incredulous, Nathaniel, as is every soul worthy the name of skeptic, was ready to be convinced, was ready to go to any pains to find out the truth. It is for the scoffer, the infidel to refuse to examine and believe the truth; not so the skeptic. He stands to try the case. And he alone is the true man who will neither believe nor disbelieve without considering.

So when Philip, in answer to his doubt, says, *Come and see*, we find him immediately leaving his retreat and following. When Jesus saw him coming and said of him, Behold an Israelite indeed in whom is no guile. "After this," one might say, "Nathaniel should have believed." But faith in the Messiah was something more to such a man than the acceptance of commendation. He could not yet give him the high veneration and simple faith which alone were, he felt, worthy his own soul and the *true* Christ. He asks still, "Whence knowest thou me?" But when Jesus told him that he had judged him thus from the devotional scene under the fig-tree, and he felt that he who professed to be the Messiah, was one who judged men, not by seeming or usual standards, and that he esteemed him a true Israelite not because of the Law or Circumcision, but because he went alone and was guileless,—he felt that the true man had come; and Jesus and Nathaniel met as eternal friends,—met, by divine necessity as atom meets atom; and he found in Jesus a true friend, because, in the best sense, a *tried* friend; and Jesus found in this doubting Israelite one who never deserted him, who left all and followed him, who was with the last who saw him on the Earth!

Rabbi! thou ART *the Son of God, the King of Israel!* Ah, my brothers, the man who has never gone through the tears and anxieties of doubt, who has not been led to wander alone thoughtful and inquiring, knows not the thrill of joy with which any high certainty bursts upon an earnest spirit! He alone knows the real joy of home and fatherland who has long been separated by land and sea,—who has past through storms, perils, fears. Ye who have not felt these know not the full magic that lies in the sacred threshold of home. All joy needs sorrow for its background; all belief needs doubt.

I know when the word skeptic is mentioned, vague images of dread arise as spectres in the mind. Men think of such names as Rousseau, Voltaire, Hume. And in nothing have the vulgarity of the pulpit and the ignorance of the crowd been more displayed, than in holding up these as the types of skepticism. These men were not skeptics; at least, that was not their real and prominent trait. Rousseau had really a lack of faith,—not alone in theological dogmas, but in virtue. His Philosophy is of man,—*to enjoy;* of woman,—*to please.* But the skeptic must have faith in virtue and God; and his doubt is only of those things wherein men say that God and Virtue inhere. If he gives up the objects of reverence, he does not give up reverence itself; and his Love endures, when the temples in which it worshiped have one by one crumbled, as investigation has gone on. Nathaniel does not inquire, mark you, *Can there be any good?*—but, *Can any good come out of Nazareth?* It is not the good he doubts, but only the Nazareth.

And the skeptic's idea is not that of Voltaire. The

one is an anxious search for truth—the other, scoffing and *persiflage*. How different was the spirit of Voltaire when he said, as some one spake of Jesus, "*I pray you let me never hear that man's name again*"—from the eagerness with which Nathaniel obeyed the request of Philip, *Come and see;* and when convinced was ready to leave all and follow him.

Nor is it the skepticism of Hume which we commend. He was, however, far nobler than the rest, and his brilliant culture and excellence of character we can all admire. Yet Hume made doubt the object—to be certain of nothing, the highest condition of mind. But the Christian skeptic only accepts doubt as the means whereby he is ever climbing from doubt to greater and more beautiful certainty.

When will the world learn that it is only strong faith which can make *skeptics*. When men doubt, and suffer and die for their doubt, as they have done over and again, surely this would seem to require some faith. There is more faith even in religious error, than in the truest of inherited creeds. For none are so little in peril of thinking erroneously, as those who never think at all; and no one will ever be a religious skeptic, who has not enough faith and interest in the subject to search into it, and see that there *are* doubts connected with it, as with everything under Heaven; and who would be unwilling to spend his life, if need be, in conflict with the hard ore, simply from the higher value he places on the pure gold it holds.

After all, skepticism is only the garment of faith. The great skeptic is always the great believer. And he who has a faith which absorbs his nature, which fills his mind and life, as the sap in the tree fills the smallest veins of ten thousand leaves; he, I say, having this faith, can only speak it out in a series of skepticisms and paradoxes. When one states the deepest thing he feels on a subject in any company, there is always an ominous silence, which hints that your faith has clothed itself in perilous language.

After the timidity that is inspired in some minds toward bravely encountering the highest questionings, arising from the idea of its reprobation by scripture, and by Christ; then from associating therewith certain reprehensible characters; — spectre third rises in a horror at certain names. The Goddess Yoganidra, whom the Orientalists believed in as the illusory and beguiling power of Vishnu, in modern times has worked in the power of names, which are made to serve for facts, which they are not, and, except by analysis, often misrepresent. Such names as Skeptic, Heretic, Freethinker, Latitudinarian, have been hung up as scarecrows in the Lord's vineyard. Many have been frightened thereby from the richest fruits of thought and experience; even as some ancient tribes knew nothing of fruits of the nut kind, or of shell-fish, thinking them altogether as hard and solid as their shells. But even these names, when divested of cant meanings, contain rich kernels. What does Latitudinarian mean? Why, one whose sentiments are broad and liberal: who will not bind to any dogmas of his own the salvation or excellence of others; and will admit the possibility that he may omit seeing one side of the sphere, while he looks at the other.

Skeptic means, as we have seen, *one who considers;* and there is no more terrible satire on what the Churches have given men to believe, than the fact that the word skeptic has come to be almost synonymous with infidel; that is, *considering* these dogmas is the sure way to reject them!

The same may be said of the word *heretic.* It is simply ἁιρεω, to choose; and signifies one whose own reason and conscience, and not those of another man or set of men, have decided what he shall or shall not believe. And that this word meaning *to choose*, should popularly mean an unbeliever, simply states with unconscious honesty, that men who have the choosing of their own faith, that is heretics, are rarely known to choose orthodoxy.

And yet Churches are found to blaspheme God in his construction of the necessary functions of the human mind, and to insult the noblest part of man, by circulating tracts entitled, Confessions of a Skeptic, Freethinker's Death-bed, and the like trash!

I will take you to the death-bed of the greatest freethinker who ever trod the earth. It is a hard, severe one, and there is much agony on it. A terrible freethinker's end, you may say! It is only about eighteen centuries back. That death-bed is the cross—that freethinker is Christ. Never before had a spirit of doubt been let loose with such resistless power on this earth. His doubts led him to the doctors' feet at first, where his parents found him inquiring of them in the Temple; they led him to the wilderness, to the cold mountain and the midnight air. He brought all the existing order into doubt. Pharisee and Scribe, Temple-service and Palace, Church and State bear witness that a fearful questioning of all things is at hand. Every drop of his blood is paid for free thought. Every wound in his body, as we see it there, pleads in silent eloquence that men should be large and free, and unbelievers of all untruth; that the soul should plant itself firmly on its own instincts, and hesitate forever ere it sanction what may be false, knowing that every falsehood injures somewhere! Around that freethinker's death-bed, the voices of the darkness, agony and death, cry out to Christian souls, "Be freethinkers! If you must be so with the only reward a crown of thorns, a cross your last bed, a mother's powerless tears at your feet your only sympathy, still, be thinkers and be free!"

What love of such a being as this is worthy either of him or the grandeur of the Soul? Is the love of a slave, who fears? Is a blind, unreasoning, and therefore undoubting, acceptance a fit worship to him who died for spiritual liberation?

Thou brave young man! to whom faculties are given to be the germs of other faculties that shall forever aspire to the Infinite Light, — cherish every doubt that comes of simplicity and truth! As the little polypus presently shows on it a dot, which draws to itself strength until it expands into another organized animal: so the doubt that arises is only the germ of some higher Truth that God would unlock from thy faculties. *Cherish every doubt!* To quarrel with these convulsive throes of the mind whereby new truths enter, would be to censure the fiery seethings at the heart of the world, which presently cast up through the boiling sea some fair island firm to the step of man. For there is nothing solid that was not once fluid, nor stable which was not doubted and tried. And Skepticism is the only path to a noble certainty. "He (says Lord Bacon,) who will commence with certainties will end with doubts, but he who is content to commence with doubts may arrive at certainties."

I know that I invite you to much unrest of mind, to some sleepless nights perhaps. But who would evade the Eternal Laws and say to the Spirit of Life, "Pass on! animate the world,— kindle every star; let the great Heart beat from ocean to ocean; let the power fill full every trunk, branch, twig, leaf, vein of Nature—but leave me alone to sleep! Let none of the divine currents fill me, thrill me!"

For you can write the entire history and secret of this Universe on the smallest leaf of the forest. It is *Motion and Rest.* Rest, the sleep; motion, the dream: Rest, the Economic life; Motion, its Poetry. Nature lies as the enchanted Princess in the fairy tale; Motion is the Prince who unchains her spell and restores her scepter and palace.

And these forces of the World, Motion and Rest, enter the spiritual Life as Doubt and Certainty: the twin sisters of the inward world.

For there is nothing certain save through doubt of its certainty; nothing doubtful except by the greater certainty of that which brings it into doubt. And men are ever climbing from certainty to doubt and on to certainty again,—as men go to war for a more stable peace.

Let us see that we do not too much love Rest or Certainty! The wisdom that cometh from above, saith the Book, is first pure, then peaceable. The love of the peace that certainty invites to, amid as much evil and ignorance as are in this world, is the love of death. So are we told that those who are in regions too cold for life, desire nothing so much as to sleep, and that sleep is death.

But let us on the other hand not love doubt as an end, but as a means.

This unresting life of the Inquiring soul is not fair and good in itself, but as prophecy of a higher Rest. It is thus with what we call the beauty of motion. Motion is not the element of beauty,—*but in the motion we have a succession of attitudes and rests.* The gazelle leaping over the crags presents a series of beautiful pauses. Of any one of them we should soon weary; but each movement promises a position more full of beauty than the last. And we know that the grand and noble element in the doubts of a Human Soul in its endeavors after the Highest, is the promise it gives of the attainment of Rest after Rest, upon Truth after Truth,—all to be won, *not given!*

There is beneath a great sea of darkness, but above, a greater sea of Light flowing forever downward—all-conquering Light! And into every soul some ray of the God enters, enough to warm us with love, to purify, amidst all doubts. It is certain that enough is known for a good life. Meantime that one little ray that yet dispels not the gloom, prophesies to us the perfect day, for the path of the Just is as the sun which shineth brighter and brighter unto the perfect day.

O my brothers, across these quicksands of doubt lies the strong shore of Faith; let us press on! And to thy darkest hour the vision of our earnest Christ shall surely come. Lo! over the centuries his hand is outstretched, his lips move to-day: *Courage, doubting heart, whilst thou wast yet under the fig-tree,—there in thy secret doubt and sorrow,—I saw thee: struggle on, if need be, a year, a thousand years: only be without guile, and on this formless void of Doubt the moving spirit shall bring the Eden of a perfect knowledge!*

ORPHEUS.

For the bed is shorter than that a man can stretch himself on it; and the covering narrower than that he can wrap himself in it.

The story runs that Orpheus, having had his wife Eurydice snatched from him by a serpent's bite, determined to seek her in the realms of Pluto. He descended into Hades with the lyre which he had received from Apollo, and in the use of which he had been so well instructed by the Muses, that, whilst he played, the wild beasts gave over their prey and ferocity, and even the trees and rocks, uprooted from the earth, followed him.

At the gates of Hades a note from his lyre served to silence the three-headed dog Cerberus who guarded it, and gain him admittance. Never before had a living person entered the dread abodes of death,—never had a shade that wandered there been released to life again. But when Orpheus entered where Pluto sat enthroned in the midst of the Judges, and saw his beloved wife, sad at having lost him, he commenced a strain upon his lyre. The music wrought its enchantment everywhere. The tortures of those undergoing punishment were suspended. The stern Gods of Death and Hell were softened,—and he received permission that Eurydice should return with him to life again.

This much of the fable suffices our purpose. Lord Bacon has said that "all the ancient fables might be familiarly illustrated, and brought down to the capacities of children." And there can be no doubt that such a spiritual sense is enfolded in the story of Orpheus. Hades with its monarch Pluto and its stern judges, its guard Cerberus, stand for the Senses, the earthly propensities; the Furies are Passions. The fair Eurydice is a type of the Soul, which, though heaven-born, and conscious of the life and light in the world above the Senses, where dwells the pure Ideal to which she is espoused, still sadly leads the life of earth.

Where is the Orpheus, where the lyre, which, entering into the life of the senses, shall bind them by the sweet music of the spirit; shall bid the passions cease their clamor; shall enchain the senses, silence the fierce Cerberus, and bid the soul come forth to the higher life?

It is not all music that can cast this potent spell. The birds had sang, the muses chanted, but they did not lead forth Eurydice. It was only the lyre of her Orpheus that could. And if there were any Orpheus who by his divine spell could beat down the sensuality, the earthliness of Human Life, and bid the Soul rise to its full and Godlike stature, surely we would all gladly unite to welcome him, to follow him, and feel all that within us was inanimate and hard, follow as the rocks and trees in the fable.

Christians, you know that Christianity always professed to be this power,—this divine music which could overcome all. It was given by one who came to seek and save that which was lost,—the soul that, like Eurydice, wandered in the earthly abodes, not at Unity with God. Thus it was a religion which aimed at the solution of the great Problem which in such dreams as that I have quoted had always haunted men. That is, *Christianity claims to be exactly adapted to the conditions, aspirations, necessities of the Human Soul.*

I need not dwell on the fact that the fair Eurydice *is* in Hades; that the soul *is* born in the midst of the senses, with all their allurements and sweetness. If a man has not learned that from his consciousness, he will not learn it from words. *The first man*, says Paul, *is of the Earth, earthy.* The spiritual nature is a slow growth,—the full ear that at last grows on a spire of grass. Those who maintain that human nature is pure in essence; that it is born for God and Truth, as the wing for air, do not maintain that nothing is to be done to elevate it to its high standard. The fact that the rightful heir to the throne is born, does not certify that he has become king, and, having subdued his enemies, is seated upon it. Nay, they are perhaps more keenly alive than others to the reforms that are needed to elevate the individual and the world from their low sensual condition. Our faith in human nature is a faith in its *capacity;* faith in its high *birthright* to grandeur; a desire to make it a monarch worthy of its throne.

Now, you will readily see that, if Christianity should be effectual for liberating the soul thus, it would be the grand certificate in its favor. No miracle ever claimed for Christ, no resurrection or ascension, could be such a triumph as a redeemed soul. The proof in this case which would be given to Christianity would be such as rain and sunlight give that they are the best for grain; from the fact that under them the grain grows, without them it dies. The only proper question then to ask is, Has this Christianity been found to meet the wants of man? Has it been the sunlight to call forth faith, purity, hope, love, as the flowers of Spring from his heart? Have even its severe exactions, its yoke, its cross, its burden, been only to nourish the seeds of life for their harvest; as the snow and wind are co-workers with the farmer?

And that this is the fair test of every religious system, whether it be Christianity or Mohammedanism, I will not affirm from any one's authority, but from the very conditions of our existence. *It is simply impossible that man can be worked upon by anything which does not conform itself to his entire nature.* If anything is too distant or too small to impress itself on his retina, he cannot see it. If any sound is too faint or far to strike his tympanum, he cannot hear it. So if anything would be believed, it must impress itself on his mind as credible; if anything would be loved, it must strike his heart as lovely. To say that a man can love and believe by some magic process other than the faculties to believe and love which God has given him, is to stop a man's ear and give him an ear-trumpet.

Take a savage, for instance, and suppose yourself about to instruct him in anything. Suppose you should say to him, *London is a great city.* You see it is as unintelligible as Sanscrit to him; *London* has no meaning, *city* has none. You cannot give him ideas from without; but out of ideas, pre-existing in his mind, you may evolve a combination of ideas which will understand your phrase; you may, that is, take the savage's idea of a house, or a collection of them, as he has seen them in some settlement of wigwams; you may associate these with his ideas of *great number* so far as he can gather them from seeing the stars or a forest: then enlist his idea of grandeur, drawn from a hill or other object, to represent the enlargement of a hut into a mansion or palace,—and you may combine these into an idea in the phrase, *London is a great city;* bearing in mind that he is limited to his experiences, and that the phrase would then only mean *his own hut enlarged, multiplied indefinitely and called London.* Whence it legitimately follows that, if you would teach this or any man intellectual truth, you must presume him to be an intellectual being; and unless the terms are such as convey ideas which awaken a response in his mind, they are no more than the ancient word *abracadabra*, a series of letters which were said to contain a magic word which, if discovered, would heal diseases and enrich the world.

And so religious truth or revelation can only be addressed to a being who is religious; and to preach to men who were depraved, would be as foolish as to go with old St. Anthony and preach to the fishes; for a depraved man could not understand such phrases as *Love*, *Purity*, *Faith*, *God*. A man must have some knowledge of these ere he can understand them; a Universe of love and aspiration must have opened up before him, before they could be more to him than the language of birds. Light must enter the eye before it can see anything.

You see then how fundamental is the position, that Christianity is nothing if it is not adapted to the conditions and wants of our nature. Where it would address our rational, moral and affectional nature, it must be itself entirely reasonable, entirely moral, supremely beautiful and lovely; or else, no matter if it were our guardian angel, it would flit by us unperceived, until the sense to perceive angels were given.

And this inquiry is one for every man to make. For the soul can never be so far immersed in the senses, as that no memory of its higher life shall steal over it. Eurydice was very sad, for she thought of Orpheus and his lyre. And the faintest misgiving that ever overshadows the sinful man, is the channel through which the heavenly music may descend.

——— Like a child
In some strange garden left awhile alone,
I pace about the pathways of the world,
Plucking light hopes and joys from every stem,
With qualms of vague misgiving in my heart,
That payment at the last will be required,
Payment I cannot make, or guilt incurred,
And shame to be endured.

And now, my friends, the sad fact presses on us, and I am sure I do not overstate it, that many, judging from the history of Christianity, always one full of fire and faggot, and the present condition of Christendom, filled as it is with systematic wrong; and judging too by a comparison in our every-day acquaintance of those who profess to be Christians, with those who do not—many calm men, I say, judging from these things, have concluded that Christianity *is not* calculated to develop the soul to its height; many more are often troubled with a flitting ghost of doubt, whether it, like the false systems described by the prophet, may not be a bed "too short to stretch one's *self* on, a covering too narrow to wrap one's self in;"—whether the august soul does not demand something loftier, more rational, more attractive.

And if I had only the history of Christianity and its present fruits to judge from, I should add myself to this constantly increasing class. I cannot say that it is (alone) a credential to any man I meet, that he is a member of any ecclesiastical organization. Not that I believe him any worse; but the good and bad find their level in Churches and out of them alike, so far as statistics and observation bear any testimony. So the question which was once asked Christ, assumes a far graver importance now: *Art thou he that should come, or do we look for another?*

But it is rather unfortunate that men have been much more engaged in investigating the history of the rising of their own sects, than that of Christianity itself. If we would all pause a moment, and, struck by the slight influence of our gospel over the minds and hearts of men now, instead of declaiming so much eloquent prophecy as to the advancement and future conquests of Christ's kingdom, revert to the time of its actual coming, we might find much to make us ponder; and perhaps enough to suggest a doubt whether this gospel, which has so little effect, is really *the* gospel which was to meet the wants of human nature.

Looking back over the ages we see, as in dissolving views, one scene gradually swell into another, the strange dawning of the Christian Light on the world. The first view is of a young man, his soul possessed by a lofty idea, declaring it to the people. Do men heedlessly pass it by? Is there any sign of indifference?

No there is hate, and there is love—*but nothing between them*, no indifference! In every case those who do not feel the sense of a new element infused into their lives, are those blinded by selfish interests. It is not to those hearts whose treasure is locked in some old system of Church or State, that we look in any age to see faith gushing forth as water in the desert. But what see we on the other hand? The common people heard him gladly. The fishermen leave their nets to follow him —albeit, he says, "The foxes have holes, and the birds of the air have nests, but I have not where to lay my head." The woman of Samaria with all the city come forth and say, "Sir, give us of this water that we thirst no more, neither come hither to draw." The multitude tread one upon another! One would say they recognized in his teachings something that answered the thirst of their souls; that they did not find the bed short, the covering too narrow!

What can account for this primitive enthusiasm? To see a few men of humble origin and culture, having their interests and relations in a worldly point of view, their very *selves* overpowered by the transcendent love of a single man; to whom they were not attracted by the ties of kindred, but the simple greatness of his religion: to see them following him, as sheep their shepherd; afterward scattered by the wolf of peril, but again, despite the manifest belief of many that the whole matter was to end there, gathered together with the first love rekindled, and earnestly assailing the

Pantheon which the best thought and culture of the world had reared in many ages, endeavoring to replace it with a structure far less grand or imposing to the senses and prejudices!

But see again the wonderful success! Like that tree of the East which grows to its height in the most barren wastes of the desert,—seeking not the region of verdure, but growing by the intrinsic force of its germ;—so we behold this germ of Christianity, dropped in the most unfriendly and hard soil, bursting the small jar of Judaism where it was planted, then like the mustard-seed springing up over the graves where men have buried their worldly wisdom and interests, "the greatest of all the trees of the earth."

To what my friends, can we ascribe this mysterious, all-conquering faith? Is not our power compared with this, as of those who beat the air? May we not ask with the servants in the parable, "Sir, didst thou not sow good seed in thy field, whence then hath it tares?" And the reply comes to us most surely—*An enemy hath done this.*

The enemy, first, of a worldly philosophy, discontented with the simplicity of the Christain Evangel, and wishing to engraft upon its flourishing stem the mystical opinions of the Eastern heathen teachers!

Another scene arises before us in contrast with the achievement of the simple band of fishermen, whose voice the sheep heard and knew, when they knew not the voice of strangers,—whom the common people heard with gladness. The historians tell us of one of the largest churches in the East, where on a bright Sunday morning, large numbers of people had assembled to hear the usual Christian ministrations. Their Lord had ascended into heaven nearly two centuries before, but his gracious words, instinct with spirit and life, had come down to them from those who had known the first disciples. The gospel in all its simple purity had been in their church and with their fathers who slept, and within them truly "a well of water springing up into everlasting life." But on this morning painful rumors have penetrated the homes of these worshipers, that some changes are to be made in their usual rites. Discussions in which they had not had time nor learning sufficient to participate, had been in hot progress; the changes, it was reported, were to flow from them. The eager crowd has assembled. Soon the priest comes in and takes his stand,—one excited glance is cast on the upturned sea of faces. He then proceeds to announce that it has been decided by the powers of Church and State that changes must be made in their forms of worship. Hereafter they are to worship Jesus of Nazareth equally with the Father of Heaven and earth; they are to believe in a Trinity,—which word was that moment, for the first time publicly uttered; that this Trinity means that Father, Son and Holy Ghost must be worshiped alike,—three in one, and one in Three.

And whoso doubts this is placed under the dread anathema of the church.

At hearing this, the congregation arise to their feet in great indignation and excitement. "It is idolatry," cry some; "See written up there, *Hear, O Israel, the Lord your God, Jehovah is* ONE *God!*" And the large proportion of the vast assembly left the church; the rest remained, thunderstruck and trembling.

And here was the point where the power of Christianity began its wane. Its simplicity and purity gave way to mystical rites, and a language unintelligible to the people. Many a poor man left the pompous and costly rites of the churches, and the sermon about Logos and Trinity and Vicarious Atonement, which were the stones offered those who asked for bread, and wandered sadly alone to think of what joy those had who sat at his feet on the Olive mount, or heard him say in full rapture with the *simplicity* of the truth, "I thank thee, O Father, that thou hast hid these things from the wise and prudent, and hast revealed them unto babes."

Men whom fire and sword had not affrighted, who had followed Christ when the great and selfish interests of the world were arrayed against his Church, taking up the burden of St. Paul who cried, "Nay, in all these things we are more than conquerors through him that loved us,"—such men as these were sent forth affrighted by a single word! They could suffer, but were afraid to be false to themselves and to God;

no! they would not worship Three in One more than they would a square circle! Never up to that time had the church used force on the people. So great was the privilege and so dear, that the force was on the side of the enemies of the Church to keep them from being Christians. But coeval with the date of the mystic dogmas is the history of the sword in the church. A great painter before that time had painted an ideal image of Theology, as a beautiful, merciful virgin, crowned with the white rose; but now blood reddens the white roses, and they fall, leaving nothing but harsh thorns to crown Theology. Every tie was sundered between the people and that church they had loved so well to call their "dear Mother." The bed was too short,—the covering too narrow.

A brief while suffices for another view to arise. We have here a large and costly temple, full of ceremonies; Bishops, Priests, Cardinals clad in strange and fantastic garbs; no less strange doctrines; the worship of angels, and saints, and images; the Madonna and child are more prominent than anything else. Preaching and reading of the sacred records have given way to genuflexions, and crossings, and holy water. Alas! compare this with Jesus teaching on the sea of Galilee! How far have we come from that? Is this what the common people would gladly hear?—this what is adapted to their necessities? No, my friends! It took a terrible power, the power of fire and faggot, now and forever, to retain it. Ask why the numerous and fearful paintings of Hell and its torments fill so much larger a space in their churches than any others? It is because it was found that the people did not LOVE the Church; so adhesion thereto must be secured by terror and threats. But Jesus did not threaten. Never! When his disciples would have called down fire from heaven on the unbelieving Samaritans, he rebuked them and said, *Ye know not what manner of spirit ye are of; for the son of man is not come to destroy men's lives but to save them.* How his voice must have sounded in the ears of the persecuted dissenters, full of the depth of prophecy: "I am the good shepherd, and know my sheep, and am known of mine. And a stranger will they not follow, for they know not the voice of strangers."

And to-day that church stands before us claiming to be the true Church. I know that it is customary very hastily to denounce it. But let us pause a moment: Because the history of this church has been one of persecution and intolerance, is really not an argument against the theory on which it is founded. All other churches have been guilty of bigotry and intolerance, and if they had been as old as the Catholic Church, they would have shed blood too. The world was undeveloped, and why should the church not be? It would prove just as easily that the world is God's blunder, because such things took place in it, as that this church is necessarily false on that account.

It will not do to despise the claims of the Catholic Church. For we have seen in our own day men of high genius and superior cultivation—such men as Newman, Pusey, Brownson, Froude—seeking rest for themselves in that church ; laying down all the dearest interests and associations of life, and the highest positions in their respective churches, to become obscure worshipers in the Romish Church. Now I, for one, believe in the excellence and sincerity of these men ; seeing no reason to doubt them.

This much is certain, *No thinking man ever began to examine the grounds of his faith who did not find much that was of doubtful strength therein.* And, the more it be investigated, the more does it come to resemble the question asked Simonides by Hiero, *Who, or what is God?* We are told that the philosopher asked a day to consider, and at the end of that, another, and at the end of every day, another; the difficulty increasing in exact proportion to the thought bestowed upon it. A fool can ask more questions of every church on earth than its wisest men can answer in a life-time. And in Protestantism every man has these questions urged upon him personally.

What wonder if one, having searched into these things, and found that though he may escape the more obvious difficulties, may solve the nearest problems, he thereby only enters into the region of new ones ; as in the progress of our planet some stars set behind us only that others may rise: what wonder, I say, if one shall find this endless search painful, and shall long for some rest for the weary and perplexed brain. "Right bravely, O my brothers, did I start with you. I had found what God was not—that he was not Triune, nor wrathful, nor capricious; but what God is, I know as little as ever. And here is the vast problem of evil in the world unsolved. I must rest. The way is hard and bleak."

Then comes the voice of the Church—tender, affectionate:

> Joy of the desolate, light of the straying,
> Hope when all others fail, fadeless and pure.

Think no more, O man, of these vast things. Thou canst not know them. Thou wilt only vex thy heart, and waste thy energies. God has established a Church to study deeply things for which thy daily cares allow no time; trust them to us and be it enough to do thy duty. Already thou art perplexed and sad—come! rest thy heart on the breast of her who is thy Holy Mother!

But no! the soul cannot rest there! The Holy Mother finds no children more perilous than her new converts; so fearfully consistent and childlike are they. In a moment of weariness or doubt they may flee thither; but a soul which has once been addressed by the Eternal Best can never rest long. So have I seen a bird beaten from its flight by some sudden storm and wind; but when it has past over, the wing again strikes the air and it passes on into the blue heaven.

A rosary, a crucifix, a wafer, even if it be the body of Christ, cannot satisfy an immortal spirit. The bed is too short for one to stretch himself on it; the covering too narrow for one to wrap himself in it.

But when the spirit has decided thus—decided that she cannot rest on the venerable couch whereon the Holy Mother soothes her children, think not her pinion will stay at any height short of the summits bathed in the pure ether of her own Ideal. Thenceforth she has become sophisticated, and detects the least remnant of externalism and cant that linger or lurk in any church which opens its arms. To every creed which claims the devotion of the soul it cannot satisfy, untwining if need be the closest arms of affection, "No," she cries, "I am not my own: Thou, God, hast made me for Thyself, I cannot rest but in Thee! Sound thy voice, O Truth-spirit, I follow thee; I am determined to press endlessly to thee!"

Stand forth! cries the now insatiate questioner to the churches; and of each as it appears the Spirit ever asketh: Is your bed fit for the awful majesty of the human soul? Does it allow for its infinite expansion? Does it remember that a soul is never at unity with itself unless it *grows unceasingly*—wiser in each moment than it was the past moment? Is the bed long enough for a man to *stretch* himself on it? Does it anticipate the tremendous possibilities of excellence which beckon us — heights overleaping heights forever; to which, though they be spiritual air-castles, the soul can never cease to aspire without losing its inherent nobility, and having its white wings trail in the dust, its garlands wilted?

Again she saith to the creed, Stand forth! Is thy bed long enough for one to stretch thereon his mysterious *self?* Remember, it is not whether it suited the soul and stature of Augustine, or Luther, or Wesley, or Fox, or Calvin, or Channing: can it satisfy every soul that can be born? Away with the old faith which would mould every spirit to one rule of development; squaring all by cant phrases, such as justification, adoption, sanctification. Every soul must have *its own* regeneration—one adapted to its special temperament. Rules about this, thank God, have always been ropes of sand. More generous is the text of the old Persian Bible, "The paths to God are as numberless as the breathings of created beings." Can *every* man, then, find your bed long enough for himself; find his individual insight and force faithfully and fully represented? If otherwise, your creed is as the fabled bed of Procrustes, to suit which the limbs were to be drawn out by cords or lopped off, as was demanded.

Or is your bed a bed of roses, without one leaf doubled, lest the slumber of some oblivious soul should be roughened? Is it a series of assertions which interest me not; of which you know nothing, save that men have always said so; assertions which do not fill me with tremendous conviction and joy, causing my spirit to leap forth as a sword from its sheath, athirst for victory on life's battle-plain?

Know, O man, that the soul is a god, and ever says to all short of God, There shall be none other before me! Nothing partial and low shall mix her pure wine, or temper her divine intoxication! Her divine right it is to bring all institutions and creeds to her bar. For they change and pass away with the growing world, but the soul remains and shall not pass away!

And from this faith we shall not be driven by any weariness; for to answer this, the subjects are the highest and most joyful which ever enlisted human powers. Nor by any ill success in the search for truth in its highest forms: wonderful indeed if the soul *did not* come short of its aim—the aim is so high. See the enormous design of religion! It is to search for the ways of God to man; it is to seek for the secret of rapture so divine, that man shall partake of angel's food: it is to know God himself! If the soul were less grand, it would have less disappointment; if its mark were low, it might be reached. But no; rather let us be ever vainly striving, than be content with what is partial; for if you will be content with the *mediocre*, that you shall get—but nothing more.

Defeat and failure then are not signs of weakness, but of strength, of nobleness; they teach us not to despair, but spur us to greater effort. For the soul of man must forever rise up toward that grand stature which the heaven of stars hint as they silently await the time when they shall crown him King; it must rise to a Beauty that shall find the beautiful Nature his handmaiden; and, until he reaches this, it must be written of all the creeds that he may adopt for a moment; of all the churches wherein he may kneel for orison or vesper; of all but God mirrored in his universe, mirrored still more in the pure heart, The bed is shorter than that he may stretch himself on it; and the covering narrower than that he can wrap himself in it.

THE MINISTER.

THE Son of Man came not to be ministered unto, but to minister.

IT is related of one of the Fathers of the Desert, that, on one occasion, when he sat meditating on his Lord, in devotion to whom he had separated himself from the world, and praying that he might have some sign that his devotions were accepted, one side of his cell seemed covered with a white haze. As he gazed, a form appeared, and, glancing at the face, he saw that it was Christ, dimly seen indeed, but with the face and attitude which accorded with the traditions of the Church. The figure was indistinct, and sometimes he doubted if it was there; then again it would glow a little. His heart filled with joy: he fell on the floor before the vision. "O, my Lord!" he cried, "for some manifestation of whom I have so longed, dost thou then come at last to bless me, ere I depart?" As he gazed up, half-blinded by tears, at the vision, the bells of a neighboring convent sent forth their evening call for alms. It was at that time, that the needy came to the convent-gate, to receive what Charity would distribute. The good Father had never failed to be there with his mite for the needy, his word of comfort, his oil and wine, for the body, or the soul. The afflicted and poor had learned to look for his coming with joy. But now, he thought, how can I go and leave this, the one heavenly vision of my lifetime! It will surely fade, for the way is long. No, I will stay, and worship my Lord; I will not go, and slight his manifestation of himself.

But when he had decided thus, his heart was not at ease. He could not keep out of his thoughts images of the sad eyes, that would await his usual coming with eagerness; of chilled firesides, and children crying for bread. He could no longer stand it; but, hastening on account of his delay, he got together what he could spare of his little store, and kneeling before the vision, bade it farewell, and went forth weeping into the evening, knowing he should not see it again.

At the convent gate, he found a poor brother of Christ's, of whom he had said: "If ye do it to him, ye do it to me, whether it be good or evil;" and he relieved his want; and there were many women with little children, who kissed, with tears, his bountiful hand.

When he returned, it was night. The vision was not seen, indeed; but, as he was about to strike a light, his cell was filled with a celestial brightness, and out there stood the form, no longer dim, but clear as the sun; no longer did the face and form assume the attitude of church pictures,, but the tender smile, and divine eye, were bent *on him;* and as he fell there, nearly paralyzed, before the stupendous vision, the divine hand lifted him up, and a voice of celestial music said: "Hadst thou not gone, I had gone, indeed!"

It has seemed to me, that the good Father's experiences, which have taken this sensuous form, represent the truth of to-day. In all Christendom, there appears, not without some brightness, a face and person whom men and churches worship as Christ. It stands there, in the twilight of manifold creeds and sermons. And churches and men think, that their sole duty is to stand before that dim form and face, which are not glowing yet into expression, and never leave *that*. A thousand clear bells may ring on around them, calling them to the gates of the world, where practical duties are clamorous for accomplishment. The poor cry: "We are chilled and starving;" the laborers cry: "Our brains are growing to wood and stone; we pass through God's fair world, and know not the message of even a blade of grass;" the enslaved cry: "O God! we have no brothers, nor sisters, nor fathers, nor mothers, nor children, nor selves. Might we only die!" These all crowd at the alms-gate. Hark! it seems the convent bells ring out very loudly to-day! . . But how still within are the Christians, with and without surplices; sitting in sanctity before their historical Christ-image! Strange that they should be content to know that he smiled tenderly upon Mary

Magdalen, and wept for Lazarus, and should not wish to see his tear and smile *upon them;* and the face does not glow distinctly enough for that. They do not appear to hear the bells! They sit occupied in speaking about their image, speculating on its personality; whether it is the very substance of its original or not; whether this dim form they see has a soul, or is it a spiritual body; while for any special expression on its face, or word it utters, the Christ-figure, which Christendom sees as dimly as the anchorite saw, might as well be dead. Indeed some *do* laugh and say there is nothing but an illusion.

O, if they would only heed the bells which call them to the gates! If they would only heed them as, with deepening tones, their voices call: Christians! if ye would be like him who came not to be ministered unto, but to minister, arise and go hence! No longer let him minister to *you*, as a means of wealth, and as a tree fruitful of bishopricks, and ingenious speculations, nor as a subject of literary leisure; but go forth and minister to the needy and desolate. If ye remain when the bells call to earnest duties, then will he go indeed and entirely: once for all, and again, he sends you forth, saying: Go ye into all the world.

O, what bright gleams of spiritual light would flash down amidst such labors! And how, when returning into our church altars from such practical employ, the before dim form and face of the historical and traditional Christ, would glow with life, and a tenderness beam on the super-sensual eye, and his voice speak in the hearts of us, with the ancient thunder which so roused the long slumbering echoes of Palestine!

We appear to have forgotten the second coming of Christ, as a prophesy yet unfulfilled; that he must first come as historical and personal, and afterward in the complete success of every principle which he ever uttered. We think him dead. But a little entering into those principles of justice, truth, love, and freedom, and some effort toward their practical adoption in the world, will cause the living Christ to flame forth before you.

> Nor times shall lack when, while the work it plies,
>   Unsummoned powers the blinding film shall part,
> And, scarce by happy tears made dim, the eyes
>   In recognition start! *

He said, "I came not to be ministered unto but to minister." It is the Key to that life, and, alas, it is to be feared, to that alone. The *ministry of self* assailed him as strongly as others. "All these," said Selfishness, "will I give thee if thou wilt worship me,"—as he gazed on kingdoms and realms which his superior powers could so easily grasp. But he came not to be ministered unto; and so had no crown but of thorns. The *ministry of self* came in the form of the wealthy, who, we are told, pressed him to go with them; but he came to minister to the poor, so he could only say, "The foxes have

* A. H. Clough.

holes and the birds of the air have nests, but the son of man hath not where to lay his head." When he was in the temple, they wished to minister to him if he would forego his own ministry. But when they gave him the book of Esaias, he read, "The Spirit of the Lord is upon me, because he hath anointed me to preach the gospel to the poor; he hath sent me to heal the broken hearted, to preach deliverance to the captives, and recovering of sight to the blind, to set at liberty those who are bruised, to preach the acceptable Year of the Lord." He then announced that he was come to work this ministry for all nations. Then were they all filled with wrath and thrust him from the synagogue, and carried him to the hill-top in order to cast him headlong. The youth escaped: yet still, did he continue that life which, whilst it sought no ministry from others, neglected nothing that would bring joy to any human heart. None were too poor for relief, none so obscure, but he would find them, none so degraded but he would elevate them. His life was perfect because it was full to the requirement of his age, and was adequate to every emergency. And such a life, whenever lived, becomes as much a component part of the religious world, as any element becomes part of the physical or intellectual world. What becomes of life without oxygen? What becomes of philosophy without Plato; or of poetry without Homer or Shakspere? What is Religion without him who came not to be ministered unto, but to minister? Say what philosophy may, we may only consent that religion shall become abstract and theoretic, when evil has become abstract. At present, it is fearfully concrete; and we need workers of a strength terrible as the strength of wrong; and we need that in Christ such men should see that such strength is the possibility of man, and so work with him, and like him "overcome the world."

It is at the first view sad, that in this world whereinto we are born, so many things teach man, that he has come hither to be ministered unto; so few that he has come to be himself ministrant. Love meets him at the beginning, and weeps over him at the end of life. He becomes dimly conscious even in childhood that he has been born heir to the vast estate of parental affection. He grows to have his boyish wants provided without thought on his part, and all his foibles tolerated. He grows to find, as a young man, that millions of money and contrivances have been employed for centuries to make royal roads to learning for him, and to surround him with preventives to *ennui*, before inner resources are fully opened, by music and dancing, and agreeable romances, adapted to the hey day of his blood.

Every age unlocks a new world of charms. Man finds himself born into a planet glittering with spires, domes, towers; every zone loads him with spices, fruits, or treasures. "For thee (cries a Poet) Naples,

Florence and Venice, for thee, the Mediterranean, the sunny Adriatic; for thee both Indies smile; for thee the hospitable North opens its heated palaces under the polar circle; for thee roads have been cut in every direction across the land, and fleets of floating palaces with every security for strength, and provision for luxury, swim, by sail, and by steam, through all the waters of this world.*

It were wonderful, perhaps, if a man did not assume, as granted, that the end of existence on earth was to be ministered unto. And indeed, the world has been an apt scholar to learn this, if this be the real lesson of things. For it is not hard to say, what this age represents. You know that all ages are representative. We speak, for example, of the ages of Pericles and Elizabeth, as ages of letters; the middle ages, as ages of feudalism and chivalry; and so of others. This is the age of self-seeking. If a dead man were to rise from his grave, it would not startle us more than a real hero, if he should appear; I mean a hero such as Christ, or even Socrates, or Luther,—a man who should care so little about being ministered to, that he should be willing to be *killed;* and who should be such a faithful minister in telling others what is right and true, that they *should* kill him. This Society has often done, and will do now, if tempted by any blunt Truth-teller; for though Society

* Emerson.

loves dearly to be ministered unto, yet it as dearly loves to prescribe the way in which it shall be done.

And it is because the Spirit of Society in this age is *Selfish;* because our very intellects are being coined into money, our consciences becoming rolls of bank-notes, our souls subject to climate in their moral perceptions, which, as mercury in so many animated thermometers, rise or fall as we go north, or come south: O, it is for this that the text gathers a startling emphasis for our ears to-day; and let it ring on in thunder in every heart, where one desire may linger to be like Christ, The son of man came not to be ministered unto, but to minister!

And you need not think, any one of you, that you can evade the responsibilities of the age, or its demands. So it is, and must forever be, that each one must stand for so much weal or woe to his race. Think now, each one, if you do not know of some heart's joy which is resting on you,—which at your bidding, or failure, would become anguish. And of that one whose good is at your mercy, the same may be said: he, also, bears the happiness of others, it may be, many others, and these in their turn. So, with every man, there is a thread running out through other hearts, multiplied into a thousand influences. It is as true of the human, as of the physical world, that each movement must change so much the center of gravity of the Universe; and every step shake worlds.

The demand of every age, most of all of this age, is

for men clear-headed enough to see their posts of duty in this world, and stout-hearted enough to stand by them. It is required that they shall be men of a large faith and equal insight into the "eternal fitness of things," from the highest point of view possible to the time; and that when the Eternal Idea has addressed them in their best thought, they shall hold to that thought, as to a proper master, and follow its behests above all others; above the inducements of vast majorities. All men of success owe it to a grander servitude, and cry in the moment of triumph, Not unto us, O Lord, not unto us. They work better than they know; and the rough marble now radiant with beauty, surprises most of all him, who, by slight erasures through months, had forgotten the whole in the necessity of mediate efforts.

Brothers, the world seems perishing with blunders! On one side we see a host of men who have adopted some little fragment of a truth, itself fragmentary, and because, holding it close to their eyes, it shuts out the world and sky, imagining that it *is* the earth and heavens—see them pushing it hotly to all extremes. Golden riches, and long periods of more golden moments, and the great, strong sinews of the body, and manifold fibers of the human brain and heart, are wasted and crushed beneath every contemptible little *ism* that drives its car with gay brass-band and paint, along the pathways of the world; energies which, gathered on a few simple principles, as demonstrable as that one and one are two, would redeem the world!

It is too bad. I sometimes think the extremists are right in saying, that Ignorance should be punished. Napoleon said of an action, "It is worse than a crime, 'tis a blunder." And my brothers, in a world where so many joys and griefs depend on the action of the least of men; a life where not one scene of the heavens or earth fails faithfully to warn us of the eternal destinies of all things, and the vast responsibility of life—I say that, in such a world, no man can be ignorant, without *deep crime resting somewhere;* oftenest, I believe, resting on the State, whose duty, in the highest sense, it is, 'to plant a school-house by every fountain, and make the one as free as the other.'

But while ignorant fanaticism, or a zeal without knowledge, holds its sway on one side, on the other we find the antithetical crime, a knowledge *without* zeal, which is worse; for knowledge chilled by cowardice, narrows at last into mere cunning or bargain-tact. Numberless souls are waning, yet think they have virtue; alas, they do not see that they have not bravely gone up to the standard of virtue, but have dragged that standard down to their own dust! Never was the old Benthamism, the "doctrine of selfishness," advanced more boldly than to-day, even while the shriek wherewith it was met by the common conscience, has scarcely died from our ears. Enough men secretly doubt whether men are capable of any disinterested action.

Every nation on earth is at this moment allowing large interests, *mere interests*, to settle questions so sacred that the principles which they involve, stand as the very Throne of God; and shall stand when the interests which supersede them shall have turned to the dust, whence they have wormed their way up into the sanctuary of man's heart, and blighted vast harvests of souls which God would have garnered!

In the Church the greatest divines declare they cannot reach men but by appealing to their fears; and so goodness and spirituality are recommended as good speculations. The trail of the serpent is in the so-called highest interests of man; the animal ascends the throne, and the spiritual turns office-seeker under it.

The sad fact draws near the fountain of tears. Backward! backward! into the old days of which it is written, "this was the reign of fish;" "this of reptile;" "this of mammal;" and shall it needs be that a higher race must write of ours, "this WAS the reign of man?" Selfishness is the legitimate efflux of the animal nature, and God will not have the world ruled by the animal. The creative power is not spent!

And the Christian need not conceal his faith and hope that such a new race has been begun, and shall increase in numbers and power, until it overrules the animal, whether it be on two or four feet. A race of those who see something in this universe beyond an infinite trough or larder; something beyond a universal wardrobe, or banking-house, or endless dancing-saloon;

men who have bread to eat that the animal knows not of; whose treasures are incorruptible. Lo! a new race, possible if not historical, conceived *every one* of the Spirit, born of a Virgin, suffering under Pilate, dead and buried, ascended into the heaven of self-forgetfulness. Need I say, that the Adam from whom the new race hath sprung, is he who called himself the Son of Man—the child of our real manhood—who, in a self-seeking age, and to all self-ministering men, said: "The Son of Man came not to be ministered unto, but to minister."

My fellow-man! look into this world, look into thine own heart, and tell me if there is not something new and startling in this rumor of the advent of a man, who preferred ministering to others to being ministered unto? I do not wonder, that the old Christians, when they read the record of his ministry; of his constant self-renunciation and self-forgetfulness; of his tenderness with Mary and Martha, Judas and Peter, and the woman taken in adultery; of that bountiful nature, which, as some sweet south wind of spring unbinds the frozen streams, and causes nature to smile again in flowers, made the human heart gush again with joys long sunken, and warmed into fragrant life all of virtue or beauty which the human heart contained;—I marvel not, I say, that the ancient fathers, as they read, and heard, and conversed of these things in the life of Jesus, called him the *Logos*, or Divine Word, the traditional emanation of the Deity, which was said to have created the world. Surely there is every reason to see in him the same spirit which created this world. I know of no two things more alike than the Spirit of Christ and that of Nature; for Nature also comes to minister to us. See the sweet circle of charities; how the revolving seasons fill man's horn of plenty; how beauty flames in on every sense; how pearls, and gems, and metals enrich man! And to the discerning eye, Christ is in this charmed circle; he also bears the fruits of all life's seasons, from early childhood to maturity; he too fills the higher senses by the beauty, the music, the fragrance, the sweetness, the solidity of his life; and if all the pearls, and gems, and gold were fused into one, who will say that it would weigh beside the pearl of price, Purity, which he brought us? Truly, "without him was not anything made, that was made."

And shall not we also, my fellow-men, join in with this charmed circle of Christ and Nature; feeling, as thus alone we can feel, the currents of the divine life? I do not believe that the Church has yet *dreamed* of the vitality and life which await her, when the celestial springs of Charity shall have been unsealed in her borders—when it shall have surrendered itself a channel for that love which overcometh the world. The genius hovers above us, but cannot fully descend into our communion, till Christ, the man, is more fully realized there; till to the cry of the poor, the weak, the wronged, the Church, with no hesitant voice, responds: In God's name, we will save you! Hang your whole weight upon us; ye shall not sink, but we sink with you! Then may we expect it when other virtues and sins are preached and rebuked; when the questions asked are not, Does he go to church? Does he say his prayers?—but, Do the blessings of those who were ready to perish fall upon him? when, instead of creeds and confessions, hung upon the walls, graven on the child's heart, shall be the noble creed of Manzoni:

All made in the likeness of the One,
All children of one ransom,
In whatever hour, in whatever part of the soil,
We draw this vital air,
We are brothers; we must be bound by one compact:
Accursed he who infringes it;
Who raises himself upon the weak who weep;
Who saddens an immortal spirit!

THE PENITENT.

THEN Judas, who had betrayed him, when he saw that he was condemned, repented himself, and brought again the thirty pieces of silver to the chief priests and elders, saying: "I have sinned in that I have betrayed the innocent blood." And they said: "What is that to us? See thou to that." And he cast down the pieces of silver in the temple, and departed, and went and hanged himself.

TO EVERY human consciousness is opened a sense of the two vast possibilities of our existence—the higher and lower—which we commonly term good and evil—Heaven and Hell. These are Nadir and Zenith of the spiritual world. And all histories, whether of men or nations, may be classified from this inward and universal growth of the tree of the knowledge of good and evil; for as the Tree of Life has bloomed into our human world, so has Evil flourished, and borne to all ages the harvest of wrong.

But these do not concern us very much, except as they appear in the private heart, and personal life. These white and black spirits seem to have their incarnations in our midst. You know that it is an ancient idea, that men come into the world with constitutional tendencies to certain things, to which they seem bound, as representatives to their constituencies. In the moral world, there would appear to be larger generalizations. And while we cannot classify men into the good and bad—no one being either altogether good, or altogether evil—yet it would seem, that, on one hand, men may so strive upward, as to be caught up by some superior force, which overcomes the earthward gravitation; and, alas! it cannot be denied, on the other, "that as there is an inspiration of holy love, so there is an inspiration of hatred or frantic pleasure, with which men surrender themselves to the impulses of destructiveness; and when the popular language speaks of possessions of Satan, of incarnate devils, there lies at the bottom of this the grave truth, that men, by continued sinning, may pass the ordinary limit between human and diabolic depravity, and lay open in themselves a deep abyss of hatred, which, without any mixture of self-interest, finds its gratification in devastation and woe." *

These thoughts press upon us, as, from the swarming millions of the generations, emerge two figures; one bearing on his face the light of God—the other, this evil shadow, both necessarily associated; and the character of each brought out into fullest relief by the inevitable contrast. There they stand, face to face, Judas and Christ.

There was a painter, who, walking the streets of Florence, saw a child so lovely, so beautiful a picture

* Müller,

of purity and heaven, that he asked and obtained permission to paint its portrait. He placed it on his wall as a type of innocence—as something which should remind him of a sphere in which humanity could exist. In the course of time, he was anxious to paint another face, from life, which should go beside it in his studio, and which should represent all the dark and evil passions of human life, as entirely as the child's face did purity. They should be his symbols of Heaven and Hell. A score of years passed, and the painter found no such demon-face. But on one day, passing through a prison, he saw in a dungeon the face he would paint; it was the face of one condemned to death for a fearful crime. That face, all written over with darkest histories, he put on canvas, and placed beside the child's, which he had taken years before. Then flashed on him the terrible fact, which was afterward confirmed, that the demon and angel were one; that he had painted the childhood and manhood of the same person.

As we call forth, and hang upon the heart's walls the portraits of Jesus and Judas, let us know that they are two phases of the same being—man; so does the same earth rise into mountains, and sink into caverns. If in Jesus we see a human soul, purified of earthliness, soaring to the sun, claiming his divinity, and sitting at the right hand of God, in Judas we see a soul in descent; the dark shadow of the earth stealing over its brightness, showing the tragedy of earth and heaven, a soul's eclipse.

I have not selected this subject without hesitation. Is it best, on this one free day of the week, when we would fain forget the baseness of common life, and the treachery and selfishness we meet there, in this dear retreat of the spirit, the Sunday; where we would seek out rather that part of the sky which is cloudless, and lose ourselves in its pure depths—is it best, on this day, to trace that dark vein of evil which starts out from the name of Judas?

It would seem necessary, that we should adhere to the natural history of the soul. What would we think of a naturalist, who, instead of reporting what he found in nature, should theorize as to what might have been; instead of adhering to things as God has made them, to the smallest *antenna*, should indulge in fancies of genera and species, which do not exist? Our true theme here is, *man as he is*—the evil man is included equally with the saint.

It is a maxim left by Goethe, that "nature reveals her secrets in monsters." Some of the leading laws of physiology have been discovered by a close attention to monsters. Also, if there be monstrous out-growths on the soul, and we shall probe them, not with morbid curiosity, but earnest devotion to truth, we shall find in them high revelations. Let us loathe nothing. There, in the dung-heap, the chemical laws work on as much as in the painting of rose and violet.

Of Judas, personally, we know but little. As his name, Iscariot, indicates, he was a native of the City of Kerioth, and is said to have been "the son of one Simon." Jesus called him to be his disciple in all good faith, and Judas followed him manifestly in the same spirit. Finding him apt in pecuniary affairs, Jesus appointed him the bearer of the purse, which they all had in common, and which sufficed for the few and simple wants of the disciples, and was the means of their charities. This position, which might have enabled Judas to realize the high saying of Christ, that it was "more blessed to give than to receive," was transformed by himself into a curse. It seems to have been the means of the first excitement of avarice in him. You will readily recur to that touching scene with Mary:

"When bringing every balmy sweet
The Eastern climes afford,
She at the Saviour's hallowed feet,
The precious ointment poured."

There where he sat, at meat, in the house of Simon, the wealthy Pharisee, in before the amazed company burst the weeping Mary, and broke the alabaster as her heart was broken, and poured the precious nard, as her tears were poured. All seemed enfolded in a hallowed silence, as she knelt at his feet, bathing them with her tears, wiping them with the hair of her head. Judas was the only one hard enough to break that holy silence. "Why," he muttered, "was not this ointment sold, and given to the poor?" The conclusion of

John is inevitable: "This he said, not that he cared for the poor, but because he was a thief, and had the bag."

This seems to have been the first incident which roused, in any of their minds, a suspicion of Judas. They do Christ little honor, who seek, on the force of a few doubtful texts, and to support the useless idea of his omniscience, to make it appear that he had a supernatural knowledge of Judas' wickedness, and his design to betray him, from the first. Could Jesus consistently have taken into their fellowship a man of such evil purpose, had he known it? Could he have given him the money-bag, had he known that his besetting sin was avarice, and thus been the means of his temptation, while he taught *them* to pray: "Lead us not into temptation?" No, friends; in the attempt here to "make out a case," as the lawyers say, for some mystical plan to be carried out, or omnipresence or omniscience in Jesus, or literal infallibility of the Scriptures, some have imperiled the purity and truthfulness of Christ's character, which *are* essential to our reverence of him, whereas omniscience is not.

The next view to be taken of Judas, historically, is at the Last Supper. Already he had been consulting with those who sought to take Christ's life. He had accepted their proposals; but any one, who had not heard the end of the history, would follow his steps to this memorable upper chamber, with deepest interest and hope. As he enters there, an evil man, to join with pure and loving hearts, in what they all feel to be their last interview, we may look to see the triumph of good over evil. There is something in the sharing a common danger and sorrow, which knits the souls of men more strongly than they are aware of, until they try to break away from such fellowship; and we say: Judas, when he enters the circle, will feel the old love rekindled; the sacred presence will restore true pulses to his heart. There is something in the atmosphere surrounding a noble and true spirit, which withers every noxious weed of evil in those who enter it. Ah, yes, we say, when he salutes his Saviour again, and feels that eye, pure and tender, resting upon him, he shall find that he loves him still. He will melt to penitence; will fall down before his best friend, and, like Mary whom he once rebuked, bathe his feet with tears.

Alas! Judas has no eye to see that face, nor the soul which could feel that presence. "Poor depraved humanity!" some one will say; but no, surely. It is just such hardness as this, such sin as this man's, that the human consciousness has agreed to call *inhuman*, not *human*—*unnatural* actions, not *natural*. Where is he who shall say that Judas' treachery was *human*—that his kiss was *manly?* Yet if humanity is depraved, the most humane must be the most depraved. If man is evil, the manliest thing would be meanest. By calling good things *humane*, *manly*, *natural*, human language testifies the native grandeur of our nature—making evil a violation of our nature.

It was when Judas had entered and sat in their midst, that Jesus was impressed with a sense of evil near him. Presently he broke out with the startling words, "One of you shall betray me." How eagerly did each one, conscious of no such intent, cry, "Lord, is it I?" Peter, most probably in an undertone, asked John, who sat nearest Jesus, to inquire of him to whom he referred. Jesus replied, also in a low voice, that it was he to whom he should give the morsel, he then held, when he had dipped it. Judas seeing them conversing thus, and supposing they spoke of him, since he knew he was the one, asked, most probably in a half-mocking way, "Is it I?" John looked at him just then, and there is no wonder that, seeing him in a new light, he should write that Satan entered him at that moment—and, continues the simple narrative, "he then having received the sop went out, and it was night." Ah, yes, night, dark, unstarred night! For when God's light within is obscured, then falls Night, like a black pall, on all things. Who can tell the intensity of the darkness of the soul, which could pass through such a scene as that of the Last Supper, unmoved from its evil purpose! Well does the Scripture speak of the "mystery of iniquity." As in some deep cavern, when the guide casts a stone in a pit at our feet, we hear it rolling on in the awful depths for many moments, and, when we think it has surely found its rest, hear again a far distant crash in the earth's bowels, causing us to turn chilled and awe-stricken from the precipice—so when we pause, pallid at this depth which Judas has reached, what horror seizes us when the lower hell yawns, and Judas comes with the foes of Jesus, and says, "Hail, Master," and kissed him! O Judas, betrayest thou the son of man *with a kiss?* Could'st even *thou* do *so* basely! It has introduced a new phrase into human language; as yet the human mind had not conceived such a monster as a "Judas-Kiss."

But all possible pictures consist of lights and shades, and this is not an exception. We have been looking so steadily at the black shading, that we are likely to forget that there are limitations to all evil—that the Devil is not so black as he is painted. I must affirm here, that I share the grave doubts which have arisen in many minds, concerning the ordinary understanding of this sin, and its motives. For it must be borne in mind that almost every place has been assigned Judas, from the pit of the archfiend to the seat of the archangel. Epiphanius and others have preserved to us an account of the gnostic sect of Cainites, who held that Judas was an instrument in the hand of God for carrying forward the divine plan; and that he was not only blameless, but that his submission in accomplishing the most painful and disagreeable part of that plan, should gain him canonization for unparalleled sanctity. There is also a book called the Gospel of Judas, which was excluded by a few votes from our New Testament. Theophylact and others have supposed that Judas was confident that the people would unite and save Jesus, if anything were attempted against him; and therefore supposed he was getting the money without doing any harm to Jesus. German critics, always the most thorough, generally agree that Judas anticipated a result different from the actual event. And all of us have perhaps had similar misgivings. Why this surprise at Christ's condemnation and consequent agony of spirit? Did he not foresee it? Then is it probable that for thirty shekels, between fifteen and twenty dollars of our money, he should bathe his hands in human blood, and sell his soul?

There seems a strong probability that Judas shared, as for a long time did all of the early Church, the Jewish idea of the Messiah, that of his being a temporal Prince; that being continually disappointed in this, he became impatient, and wishing, or at least willing to hasten the crisis when he would either be proved an imposter or crowned king, as he supposed he would be inevitably, if he were the true Messiah, he agreed with the Jews to deliver him to them, or, at least, to point him out—which, by the way, was not a matter of much importance, as far as Jesus was concerned, since he could have been found, as he said, "daily in the temple." It did Judas much more harm than Jesus. I think, therefore, that there is little reason for associating the act with deeper guilt than that of Peter's denial; one denied for fear, one pointed him out for money: they did no special harm to Christ in either case. The horror of men in all ages, is in the crime against friendship and the ties of piety; and, in the case of Judas, it is enhanced by the unmanly and hypocritical manner of the deed, by a kiss. The human heart readily agrees with the Koran, that the deepest of the seven hells is for all hypocrites. We may conclude then very surely, that Judas had no idea of being the means of Christ's death; which accounts too, for that overwhelming agony which ended in his dying at nearly the same time with his betrayed friend.

Of what happened to him after he saw Christ led away to execution, there seems to be little certainty. In the confusion which beset the disciples, during the fearful scenes surrounding Christ's death, we can scarcely expect accurate historic accounts concerning any one man. Two entirely different reports respecting his end seem to have spread, one of which was followed by Matthew in my text, who says, "he cast down the money and went and hanged himself;" the other by Luke, who, it is thought, wrote the Acts, whose record runs thus: "Now this man purchased a field with the reward of iniquity; and falling headlong he burst asunder in the midst, and all his bowels gushed out. And it was known to all the dwellers at Jerusalem: insomuch that the field is called in their proper tongue, Aceldama, that is to say, The field of blood." Of these two accounts, (which cannot be harmonized but by pious fraud,) I think the latter has more marks of authenticity, and that there is reason to believe that Judas, instead of committing suicide, when he saw what he had done, died in some violent convulsion; probably, from the description, apoplectic, brought on by excessive remorse.

My friends, we have presented to us here a strange, awful picture—a strong, rude man, habituated to all the common hardening affairs of a life of manual labor, suddenly stricken by a glimpse of his sin, and overpowered by a repentance which nothing but death could satisfy! Around this spirit, which we have evoked to-day, cling some deep questions of the soul; let us approach them. For there is such a thing as true penitence: wherein does it resemble this of Judas—wherein does it differ from it?

I have sometimes thought it were a good Prayer, if one said, "May I have the penitence of Judas!" For see "the divine depths of sorrow" in him! Christ crucified has not so great pangs as he who helped to crucify him. Brothers, brothers, there is so much superficial repentance: a mere sentimental acknowledgment of our sinfulness in general, or in particulars; still more, a sorrow for some consequences apprehended from evil in this or another world, that we have come to think some distress of mind and begging off of hell to be Repentance. But the grief of Judas is supernatural, almost holy! In a world of shams, here is something real. As the face of Judas, leaving the Last Supper and plunging into the night, has ever been in the imaginations of men and on canvas the type of malignity, so the Judas casting down the money at the feet of the Priests in the Temple, and going forth to his wild death, has ever been, must ever be, the type of human anguish. Down across the ages sound those words wrung from a soul in pain, deeper than what we commonly feel, "I have sinned."

And see, is not here confession? Who of us really, I mean *really*, confess our sins: I mean turn away from what is evil and low in our lives, and live purer, higher lives, however much they rebuke our past conduct? Here, in the confession of this man whom all curse, we have no hollow lip-service; any one can confess he is a sinner, if only to have credit for a fine modesty. This confession *means something*, as the lightning means something. When all was danger to the followers of Jesus, when peril sprang in their fold as a wolf, and those who had followed him better than Judas, "forsook him and fled;" when Peter, who said, "Though I should die with thee, yet will I not deny thee," stood up and denied him thrice—at that time, when to befriend him is to incur public wrath, Judas the traitor, yes, Judas the Traitor comes forward, and bears witness to the innocency of Jesus, and his own sin! "I have sinned in that I have betrayed the innocent blood!" How many of us thus confess Christ and the purity of his law, when he is scourged and crowned with thorns by corrupt and violent power? bear witness to the voice of the Christ within, when it clamors for Justice, Love, Truth and Virtue?

And this penitence resembled the true in its ready restitution, and refusal of all the gain of the sin. He brought again the thirty pieces, and when they would not receive them, cast them down. There is no better test of a real repentance than whether a man is willing to give up the gains of sin; for this is practical and real. Why, it is because for this men have substituted a canting, whining, praying confession, that one is afraid to use the very word repentance, lest some one should think he has anything but utter contempt for what passes under that word. But it is only good money that is counterfeited; and no cant or error can obscure the truth, by whatever name you call it, that there is such a thing as a man's casting a steady, keen scrutiny on his whole life, and on the special acts of that life; and detecting the presence of evil in the motive and attainment, by a true repentance rising above his past, and spending his life and strength in blessing those whom he had injured or neglected: in changing his temper from bitter to sweet; in leaving bad habits and frivolous aims, for high and holy purposes of life. I would that men had more of this great penitence of Judas, reaching down to the springs of vitality, than of that which is from the throat upward.

And it is a sad truth, which must be here stated, that there are few who have no reason for this penitence. The celebrated Dr. Baxter, seeing a man borne to the gallows, said: "There goes Richard Baxter, except for grace." It was quaint, and dates from Calvinism; but we all see the deep truth which underlies. Judas is a dark possibility lurking around every one of us. Have we not a Lord Christ in Duty? Is the silver never offered us to betray that duty? He who sacrifices any principle, anything he feels is good, for earthly advantage, or pleasure, or popularity, does it take literally thirty pieces of silver to make him share Judas' sin? Usually it is for a great deal more than Judas got, and unattended by remorse and death. Dear friends, I mean just what I am saying; whatever fine resolutions we have made, and are living by now, memory still holds her wand, and evokes spirits from her deeps that will not down at her bidding—spirits of duties neglected; of guilt in thought and act; of things which shame the open day. You alone know what was the coin, and whither it went—the coin which purchased a spirit's perfect whiteness of you. *You alone*—there is another, an Infinite Eye, which sees all. Infinite Father, we give thee thanks that thou, and not we, knowest how deep is outward observance; with how many the cry of "Lord! Lord!" is a Judas-kiss, from hearts already bought over by the world!

Yet, though with one sense we might well pray for this repentance, in another it were better to cry: Save us from the repentance of Judas! It differed fatally from true penitence in some regards. For I fear we cannot ascribe a proper *origin* for it. True repentance bursts *out* from the soul, not *in upon* it. It is not born of the *results* of action. It is the conflict of a soul become conscious of the inception of sin; and although that sin may never have had any evil overt influence, (for God rules over all designs of men); may never have grown up into action at all; may have produced good where evil was intended, as is often, indeed generally, the case—yet the true penitent feels the sense of inward evil no less heavily than if devastation reigned around it. But Judas, says the record, "when he saw that Jesus was condemned, repented himself." Why should he not repent *before* he was condemned, or if he were not condemned at all? I would not like to add a feather's weight to the load of reprobation heaped by all upon him, and, it is to be feared, too indiscriminately; yet I find it difficult to trust that penitence which could pass unmoved the scene of Mary weeping at his feet in Bethany; which could slumber amid the touching scenes of the Last Supper, and invade the quiet garden where Jesus had retired for prayer; but now bursts out into despair and wild death, when the result comes, and Judas feels himself standing, with his soul naked to the eye of God, and the innocent blood of his Son upon his hands. And yet should it be remembered, that the deepest secret, in every spirit, is known to itself and God alone. Who are we that we should judge?

And that which originates wrongly ends wrongly. It is certain that Judas' repentance differed from the true in its *end;* in its influence on himself. Tragedy is not the law of the spiritual life, but triumph. There are two words used in the New Testament, which signify repentance, but of different kinds. Martineau has well translated them, as sorrow with the upward, and sorrow with the downward look. The true penitence is of the upward look; it never leads to despair; but, in losing self, finds God. See this poor man writhing in remorse, and frantically plunging the poisoned arrow deeper, even into his vitals; our good Father sends not, requires not such morbid conditions as these; they are not signs of health. It is true that deep and hot tears fall from this upward sorrow, as it passes, like a cloud, over the soul; but on those drops, which the stricken heart rains down, falls the sunlight of faith, and forth on the black cloud leaps the bow of promise. Penitence has no smile herself, but receives on her face the smile of God. Alas! Judas, when thou didst leave that best friend of thine and mine, truly "it was night," nor do we see the dawn for thee; yet God is light, and if he shall be now pouring his splendor on eyes which were blind on earth, who shall gainsay him?

Our duty is not to judge Judas, but learn our lesson of him. I would say, then, he was not moved to the *true path* of repentance, as he would have been by the unerring instinct of the higher sorrow. Whither went he with his confession, restitution, grief? *To his accomplices.* It is as the gambler flies to the card-table to retrieve the fortune he has lost there; it is as the drunkard flies to the cup to forget the misery it has brought him. What more was needed to goad his remorse into madness than their answer: "What is that to us? See thou to that." Ah! whenever we bring to the accustomed association of the world, with its pleasure and interests, our deeper, sadder moments, how soon do we find that they have nothing in common with it. "We want no earnestness, no excellence, no conscience," cries the world. "What are they to us? See thou to them."

Where was Faith then, the inner light of true repentance, touching into activity the giant in a man which plants the heel of the great human will on that serpent, which would trail through his heart, and nestle in his brain, driving off every ministering angel? Far else would such faith have led thee, Judas! They would have beckoned thee away to the scene of scourging and condemnation. Ah! could we only see thee, at this juncture, making thy way to the judgment-seat; see thee there prostrate at the feet of Him who sendeth none away; hear thee cry: "O, my Master! I have sinned in that I have betrayed thy innocent blood"— we should have something more than a vague shudder for this sad story. For *He* never said to one repentant: "What is that to me? See thou to that." Ah see! the gentle face forgets even its thorn-crown at the voice of the penitent; the very hand he had nailed to the cross is extended to the returning Judas; the very lips he had treacherously kissed, speak tenderly and kindly still: Poor Judas! even *thy* dark sin is forgiven.

O, thou great, unfailing love of Christ, "free and faithful, strong as death," could we but raise ourselves up to thee, and open up within us those immortal springs, which go forth to bless all, evil and good, just and unjust!

But the history and its moral are closed, so far as it is given me to close them; yet where human speech, feeling its weakness before the truth, which is deeper than all speech, trembles into silence, it leaves a holier voice in its place. Very much of my sermon shall be written by God's finger, when next, in your secret moment, your heart lies unfolded before Him.

We must pause far short of the depths then, and say only that Judas' penitence was remorse, which is the groan of death. As when the nervous system is shocked by some sharp pain, above its power of endurance, and cannot react and recover, but must suffer the pain to work its own consummation in death, so Judas, scathed by the lightnings of the violated law of his being, rushed wildly, blindly into the arms of Agony, to which Death was the angel of relief. But that is not hell enough for some: they have allotted him some deep and special hell, which he alone is evil enough to fill, for his sin—a sin, I say again, committed daily—nay, at some period perhaps, in every life, that of betraying Christ (with us his sacred law) for some earthly interest.

"If he that loseth his life findeth it," as Jesus said, may we not hope that this terrible agony was with Judas, the birth-throe of his higher nature, which, as one catches flame from the candle flickering in its socket, God may have caught up to burn more brightly in a higher existence? For he willeth not the death of any, but rather that all should turn unto Him and live. Surely it requires an immortal spirit to suffer so for evil conduct; a brute could not suffer so, nor an utterly hardened man.

My brothers, so great is the infinite mercy to us, let us not decide that he had none for Judas; or let him that is without sin among you, cast the first stone. His life was this: temptation, fall, remorse; what else is every life? What better claim could he have to be our human brother?

Clothed in sin and dust, we will bow with thee, O Judas! and as with expiring breath on earth thou didst bear witness to thine own sinfulness, and the innocency of thy Friend and Saviour, we also cry: "We have sinned in that we have betrayed the innocent!"

"Owning his weakness, his evil behavior,
And leaving, with meekness, his sin to his Saviour."

THE VACATION.

IT is expedient for you that I go away.

AN old Proverb says: "God is a good worker, but loves to be helped." Luther was yet bolder, and said, "God cannot do without strong men." All power is godlike, and its finitude is only degree. Our race worships force and hates weakness. The best men have agreed that weakness is abortion, nothingness; that its business on earth is to die—to fall as blossoms fall that fruits may arrive.

And yet I am sure there is no fact more universal, than a distrust of our moral strength. In my association with men, I read with pain on most foreheads, *Do not trust me too far!* A feeling of inferiority to desire and circumstance—a cowering before pressing temptations—a lack of confidence in our principles to face great passions, interests, opportunities; these constitute the chronic complaint of mankind. And, in it all, the one favorable symptom is, the prevalent strength-worship to which I have alluded. Impatience with the disease, testifies our belief that there is such a thing as health. We know that, as fabled Antæus, in his conflict with Hercules, recovered every wound and regained full strength whenever he touched the Earth, which was his mother, and was only slain when separated from possibility of contact with her, so man is the result and child of certain excellent healthful laws, in contact with which he is strong, apart from which he is weak.

To discover for this timid race, paling before the smallest clouds of temptation which rose over its sea, feeling safe only when becalmed, the solid continent of strength, came the Christ. All agree that he discovered it; but as to the direction in which it lies, there is now the greatest difference among those who hold themselves his followers. And all theories may be generalized in two. One of these maintains, that his method was to generate strength in his followers, by certain external doctrines and promises; attested by miracles, addressed to the senses. The doctrines of Immortality, of Prayer, and the like, were to do the work. His method was to guide them by his teachings, and lead them to himself. The other maintains, that all his works and teachings were designed, not to furnish a system of rules, but to clear a path for men to enter *their own* rules—not to give them fruits, but bring them to the labor which should produce fruits—not to lead them to himself, as an end, but only as a means of entering and possessing their own selves.

You see how immense the difference: the one shows God impossible to me—the other, God in me; one makes me a parasite on the oak, the other, a branch fast to the trunk; one makes my endeavors the spirals of a worm, the other opens up the ascending spheres of angelhood before me.

Can there be any doubt of the truth in the presence of the most striking of all Christ's sayings, which I have read as my text? No wonder questionings arose among his disciples, when they heard one who had fed them with angel's food, who had stretched his great self upon them, as Elijah on the widow's son, face to face, breast to breast, until they rose the only twelve *living* men in their nation—now say, It is expedient for you that I go away from you. As well, they thought, might the sun go out, and bid all eyes rejoice that it was no more!

But Christ, with his great solar eye, saw them as they could not see themselves; saw that their full strength demanded for its development, a greater self-reliance; and, as the condition of that, a weaning of themselves from that dependence on himself and his teachings, which was only adapted to spiritual infancy. When he told them that he should ere long be parted from them, sorrow filled their hearts—and in this time of their prostration, he resolved to point out their true sources of strength. "It is good for you that I go. Your true force cannot be gained from me, more than your muscles and sinews can grow strong by my labor.

If the teacher does all, the scholar will do nothing, and so know nothing; but let the teacher be withdrawn, after the task is assigned, and undreamed energies shall be born of the necessity of self-help. Thus alone, can the strength needful for your mission be supplied; thus alone shall the Comforter—which in the Bible bears its primitive meaning of strengthener—come. You yourselves have faculties which are improved by use, destroyed by disuse; and, after you are launched upon them fully, dependence on what is without, however wise, dwarfs them."

In giving this method for elevating man to his highest spiritual condition, Christ placed himself on the great facts of Nature. The highest spiritual manhood appears as the human form, as the highest result of the material world has appeared. Taking one of the lowest animal forms, we find there is no self-sustaining life. It simply fastens itself on to a rock; the water gliding by furnishes food from its sediment. It has no bone or nervous system. The sun and atmosphere regulate its conditions of life. All its life,—motions, powers, continuance,—are not from itself, but from the outward elements. A little higher in the scale, and, with the *mollusc*, the dawning of a nervous and bony structure appears—but still they exist around it as shell, not in it as centers of force. But, as animated nature rises to higher grades, the tendency is from without inward,—from dependence and imprisonment, to self-subsistence and freedom. The shell becomes skeleton—

the nerves gather to centers. And so up to man, in whom activities, once regulated by light, heat and air without, are generated within, and rule external things where lower orders were ruled by them.

The analogue in religious development is easily traced. The lowest form, Fetishism, fastens itself on a stock or stone for its god, and draws its spiritual, as the jelly-fish its physical, sustenance only from what is visible and tangible. In a higher type, such as Romanism, we see the dawnings of some independent existence. Here germs of truth, God and sacrifice, heaven and hell, are dimly recognized, though not received into the soul; they surround it only as shell, in church, pope, and confessional. The priest acts in lieu of conscience. But the progression goes on. Some higher, sinewy souls, as Luther and Calvin, draw the shell within, and propagate a race of more self-reliant minds. For awhile they are not hardy, and fully conscious of their freedom; and for a time must hold on to the external; though now it is nothing worse than some traditional cant, and an infallible book. Then begins the appearance of the true spiritual, self-helpful man on earth; with personality superior to the world and his own lower nature; able to cast away the most sacred tradition, or venerable form, if it is not adapted to his temperament; and to convert churches and creeds, sacraments and institutions, into bone and sinew, and into that divine nervous center, feebler or stronger in every man, whose fibers run out into the entire universe, and vibrate with the activities of the Infinite Mind.

It was that this divinely ordained progression, from an infant dependence to a Godlike self-reliance, might occur in those men to whom his faith was bequeathed as trustees, that he taught them to look to their separation for strength.

The Christian community, in every age, is apt to stand in the same relation to the Church, and must be warned of the same danger. I shall trust that you will not misunderstand me, and suppose me to undervalue the Church. That any people should fail to have a church representing their faith, or that, when they have it, they should be too indolent or indifferent to attend it, is the most certain indication of shallowness of mind, and poverty of character. I love the Church, and can see that, in every age, it has given signs that it may still hold, and announce the oracles of God. It is no farce that we separate from the week a sacred hour; that we make bold, in prayer and hymn, to claim personal communion with the Most High God. O! when I reflect on what all these *rest* in the human soul; what far-reaching experiences they imply; what depths the human spirit must have fathomed in its own necessities, what a universe of love and power must have been opened up to its anxious glance, ere it could build a temple or dedicate an altar to worship; then do I feel that the Church is the ever-present seal of God to man, as made in his own image; the sure title of the soul to an eternity and an infinitude for its development and felicity.

But everything that the sun shines on casts a shadow. And the shadow of the Church is, that its services, passing down from century to century, with little variety of forms, becoming the routine of generations, *may* become the routine of the individual. It cannot be disguised that many, going to church several times a week, and without intermission the year round, show plainly that their church has become an end instead of a means, and that their religious nature has no conscious existence independent of some special church. At stated times, their religion rings its bells, sings hymns, prays prayers, reads a sermon; then sleeps comfortably till the next alarm sounds.

But how do we find many of these persons, so observant of rites, when duty or accident has taken them where there is no church, no communion, perhaps not even a prayer or psalm-book, or a volume of Channing or Baxter? How do we find them when confined to the tedium of a sick chamber as their only temple?

Alas! too often the thirsty soul finds that it has left with the preacher and church that well of water which Christ said should be *in* the soul, springing up into everlasting life. This is the secret of those who have had spiritual life deepened by afflictions. We have attributed, perhaps, the graver cast to sorrow or pain; but I doubt not that it is generally the withdrawal of the usual church externalisms, on which they had relied too much. They have found that it was expedient for them, that they were left without a church for awhile. As it is said, that, at some mineral springs, those who have hobbled to them on crutches, have cast them aside on the spot, and returned with firm step, so have we seen superficial persons, with as light Sunday-thought of God diluted in a week of worldliness; or those whose religion is a mechanism of pew-hinges and knee-hinges, brought by disease or affliction into that loneliness which is nearest true strength. In resting upon themselves, they have gone into that spiritual realm, which is more than all churches, as the sun is more than any of its colors. For from the human soul, the Church first drew its life, and only from the living souls which form it, can its life become perpetual.

It is thus that often, beneath some thunder-stroke, that which was a shell of sentiment or formality, is changed to an inward bony structure of active principle; and the one-day-a-week religion transfuses all the veins and centers of every-day life. The mother of Goethe, in speaking of him, said: "My son, whenever he had a grief, made a poem of it, and so got rid of it." A true *christianized man* would have a similar power over all circumstances. He must have the alembic of a strong heart, so that each event of the day and night—the worlds of trade, intercourse, affection, grief, pleasure—cast therein, shall be reproduced as worship, and life become every whit whole and true.

Believe me, friends, the religious dealings of a week

cannot be summed up on a single day. They need a day-book as much as your other business. If this affair of the soul must be respected, it would be more convenient to carry one's preacher, Bible, hymns, and so forth, along in one's heart and head, even if one day is to be separated for the casting up of general accounts.

Have we forgotten the Ideal Man? Cannot every heart discern the life that is pure and sweet; wherein, beside the senses which receive, and the hands that work, and the common sense which so faithfully mediates between us and the world—beside and above all these, is the throne of the pure Reason, with the coronet of all virtues—never forgotten, but finding its highest good in the absorption of all the senses and faculties, over which it rules, in their specific objects?

Until the religious principle is adopted as part and parcel of our entire nature, which we can no more lay aside than brain or lungs; until it is a vital force, flowing forth with every radius of influence, and filling the circle of relations, we shall never be strong. Tender thoughts of Jesus, maxims, prayers, hymns, testaments, sermons, depend on *you* for usefulness and interest, not you on them; and if you have got into the habit of depending on them, or anything *outside* you for religious emotions, until they go away, the Comforter, the strength of God shall not abide in you.

It is not safe, then, to attribute the great differences between churches, in the frequency of their services, and the length and elaboration of them, to the apathy of the one, and the superior earnestness of the other. It may show a much higher religious condition on the side of those who have fewer prayer-meetings, and simpler forms. For it cannot be denied, that, if men were perfect, these forms and meetings would not be needed at all. All of these religious organisms anticipate a time when they shall cease. As one generation builds a temple, which another re-builds; as one age writes a creed, which another re-writes—so shall our faith and worship be enlarged; and should they reach their largest, they would disappear from without, and shine forth grandlier within. Men would bear about them, as they bear clothing, sermon and sacrament. Neither, saith the prophet, shall one, in that day, say to another, "Know ye the Lord;" for the knowledge of the Lord shall cover the earth, as the waters cover the face of the sea. Churches are signs of weakness; indications, however, that this weakness has grown sufficiently conscious of itself to cry for strength. The laws and injunctions imposed on the ancient Jews, while they were the results of the highest wisdom, show very plainly what a filthy, immoral people they were who needed such restrictions. All law is a satire. Yet Christ, in stating this principle, declared that not one jot or tittle should pass from the law till all was fulfilled. When to say, Thou shalt not murder, or steal, or commit adultery, has become as useless as to say, Thou shalt not eat arsenic; when to say, Thou shalt love the Lord thy God with all thy strength, and thy neighbor as thyself, has become as superfluous as to say, Thou shalt breathe the air, and walk by the light—then will we close joyfully our church, not for two months of summer-heat, but forever. Then the uses of a church will have been fully received; then the Comforter will have come; and man, self-poised and self-subsistent, shall be God's noblest temple; every act, worship; every thought, a hymn. And no church is worthy our trust, which does not carry within it the germs of dissolution; which does not fully see before it the gleaming goal where it ends in glorious consummation; which, regarding the necessity of outward forms as transient and partial, does not pray—

> O God, forgive our crimes:
> *Forgive our virtues too,* those lesser crimes,
> Half converts to the right.

So have I seen a stream swiftly gliding, loudly dashing, onward, onward—willing enough to turn the mill, or refresh the herd, or revive the meadow and flower in its course—but *hastening* to be lost and finished in something deeper, grander than itself, the all-absorbing Ocean!

But when I commend to you the value—even the *superior* value—of all the time in which the usual religious resources are withdrawn, as tending, not to dissipate your minds, but to cast you more fully on the inward strength—what am I doing? Am I commending to you spiritual Pride? Would I bid you be independent of the Supreme and His methods? Indeed I would not. The worship of stocks and stones were better than *no* worship. You had better depend on a rosary, a sacrifice, a book, than on self-sufficiency. That soul which is contented with *what it is*, has already died the death. But there is an interior selfhood, of which Jesus spoke when he said of the prodigal, *he came to himself*. To that interior self I call you, because it is the declared "Lord from heaven." It is that which is pained at sin; which never can rest impure; which bears heavenward. My fear is, that through the incessant routines of the Church, you may be drawn aside from that guide, and may at last have no inward life beyond the power of these forms to express. And to this point I have spoken with all the more freedom, because I know that the Church cannot be harmed one instant before it should be. All that is genuine, is safe—only the fungus need fear the probe. Abolish all the churches to-day, to-morrow they will be living with twice the former vigor. For until mankind are perfect, Conscience, that "divine curse," is abroad with loosened lash. Conscience is the master-builder of churches; the great revivalist, opening Heaven, barring Hell.

I am sure that if all churches should be closed for a year, it would enhance religious worship tenfold. For it is one of the laws of our nature, that we really enter nothing until we have held off a little from it, and then newly invented it for ourselves. This it is that makes *doubt* the necessary path to Faith. Many persons who have never doubted concerning God, Christ, the Soul, may suppose that they have faith in these; but every real thinker knows they have not. Every great truth repeats to the earnest mind Christ's words, "It is expedient for you that I go away from you," and goes, leaving the soul in doubt and darkness. It is but for a time. The soul goes forth, as Rachel weeping for her children, to seek the truth: then the old truths, which had fallen, return, not as before, but bringing their full strength with them. For though the mind receives many old truths which it had rejected, it never comes to them under the same forms and limitations as before. Under the warmth of its growing season worms have become winged. Nearly every old dogma is the grub of some golden-winged truth. The difficulty is, that men will cling to the sloughed-off shells, when the life is soaring in higher forms.

The reason of this stronger grasp of that which is temporarily removed from us, would seem to be, that, when we receive truth by inheritance or tradition, we do not see it independently, and judge it on its own merits. We see by the light of personal affection; and are often resting on the authority of parents, friends, teachers, when we think we are reposing on a legitimate conviction of the mind. So we are brought up to give a sort of adherence to what comes over the Bible, and out of the pulpit. I fear the most liberal churches have not got quite out of that. You shall find it well then for you that the Church shall be silent a little; that you shall turn away from its periodical statements to inquire of the trees, the sky, the clouds, concerning the truth or untruth of what you have been urged to accept; opening your hearts to the sacred probes of loneliness with Nature, of reflection, as to what degree of life you have distilled from all that you have heard or known of Christianity, for personal strength of character; how much is the mere husk of form.

Mark, if you please, how this law was illustrated in the case of those men to whom Jesus said, "It is expedient for you that I go away." While he was with them daily, giving them sublime truths, which they had little to do but sit and hear, they seemed to have gained no vital force from them; and, when opposition and temptation came, their purposes melted before them as snowflakes in the sun. We find—when he was *with* them, observe!—one basely betraying him, another denying him with oaths; and indeed the humiliating record had to be made, "They *all* forsook him and fled."

But see! what means this excited crowd gathered near the same place only a few months later! Is that man facing so fearlessly the enraged throng for the crucified Christ, the same who denied him before he was crucified? Can those who fled, be the same with those who now gather around the relifted standard of Christianity at Jerusalem; and those tongues, so lately dumb with fear, the same with those "tongues of flame," which leap forth, volcanic, to fuse and melt the iron fetters of Judaism, by which the people are manacled and fetlocked? Whence came this force, which, in an hour, multiplied twelve Christians into three thousand?

This was the Pentecost of great souls, when first the full extent of their labors rose before them, and no wonder-working Christ was there to relieve them. This was that super-human strength, which has been known to animate armies which have seen their leaders cut down; advancing to a victory which attested that the blows which laid them low, had made every soldier a leader, with every nerve and faculty multiplied and empowered by the pressing necessity.

I cannot but feel the lesson. I find I must often say to my teachers and to the Church, Pray, move a little. You are too strong. Pleasant enough it is to be borne in a sedan all the time; but will not that stunt the limbs Nature gave for walking? Social worship is good, but it is apt to absorb private worship; church music is good, but am I not in danger of forgetting the far sweeter melodies of silence?

Ah, I see God's full purpose, and know that Life means more than the gathering of shells and pebbles on its beach! Over the waves come the earnest voices of those who alone and in silence bore their burdens. "Into this sea, O man," they cry, "thou must plunge ere thou gain the shore of thy strength; these sturdy waves must buffet with thy God-given, and therefore, all-sufficient sinews; if thou strivest not, the waters will overwhelm,—if thou contendest bravely, they shall buoy thee bravely."

THE CHILD.

I have gotten a man from the Lord.

THIS was the exclamation of the first mother at the birth of the first child. It is to be questioned whether any of Eve's descendants have seen so deeply into the mystic nature of infancy. How many with her look upon the child *as a man;* as much so as a bud is a flower; as much so as a drop of water has the same elements as an ocean? How many see with her that the child is from the Lord; that it is indeed a "clothed eternity;" and that those little eyes were lit up at the central sun of the universe, torches of God, whose flame cannot perish? Ah, parent, elect for so high service as the care of a living soul from the heavens, I would have you bow with awe-struck Eve, and cry, I have gotten a man from the Lord!

Were one called on to vote which was the most mysterious, unexplored realm of science, he might well decide, not magnetism, but childhood. I know your naturalist, remembering how little Georgey did not think a precious fossil too good to throw at the cat, will persist that childhood, instead of being a realm of science, is the bane thereof; and literary men will all agree, that Baby is philologically derived from Babel, signifying confusion. But all phenomena of science are disagreeable until understood—comets, tides, etc., for example. And childhood is not understood, or is misunderstood.

O transcendent realm of infancy! why so guarded? The generations, as they pass, bring us orators, poets, prophets; but where is he who comes with the key of the child-soul? Who will be the "tongue of the secret," the seer—

——— the man of eld,
Whose eyes within its eyes beheld
Heaven's numerous hierarchy span
The mystic gulf from God to man!

Some clear perceptions of the depth and dignity of childhood have indeed, at rare intervals, been vouchsafed us; and there is no better calculus for the growth of the world, and the advance of God's great year, than the rising estimate of this morning time of the world.

I am glad to find, that we are beginning to read of the old theological idea of childhood with doubt. You mothers, with children in your arms, often tell me that you do not believe that parents ever regarded their babes as depraved imps. We can scarcely imagine, that the old New England divine, who affirmed, with a whole synod to indorse him, that "hell resounded with the wailings of infants," really meant just what he said. It is well you cannot believe they meant it; for it shows the strength of the sacred idea of childhood in yourselves. And yet, in estimating our growth, we must consider that these views were matters of earnest popular belief. To give you an idea of the extent of this conviction, I wish to bring before you a poem, which I came across recently. It was written in the beginning of last century by one Wigglesworth, a school-teacher at Walden, Mass., of high reputation, and was so popular, that it was used as a school-book in various parts of the State of Massachusetts. From this work, which is entitled the "Day of Doom," I propose to give you one or two elegant extracts, which refer to the children.

Wigglesworth meditates calmly on the damnation of infants:

"Then to the bar all they drew near who died in infancy,
And never had or good or bad effected personally."

There was one who, when on earth, took little children in his arms, and blessed them; we had hoped he might meet them there: Michael Wigglesworth sees, with his spiritual discernment, a change. These infants, summoned, as has been stated, to the judgment bar, commence pleading, and very rationally too, one would say, for such little folks. They cry:

"Not we, but he, ate of the tree whose fruit was interdicted,
Yet on us all of his sad fall the punishment's inflicted."

With a smile at their childish ignorance, which had not even penetrated the first volume of Calvin's Institutes—with a sigh over their altogether carnal view of the whole subject, these babes are thus indoctrinated:

> "But what you call old Adam's fall, and only his trespass,
> You call amiss to call it his; both his and yours it was.
> He was designed, of all mankind, to be a public head—
> A common root, whence all should shoot, and stood in all their stead."

Either because of the profundity of this view, or because of their good breeding, or because they could not help it, the infants yielded the point. Wigglesworth attributes it to the former; for the poem continues:

> "Their consciences must needs confess his reasons are the stronger."

They are then, according to the gospel of our worthy Michael—who seems to be a kind of forerunner of the archangel of that name, who is to trumpet the Day of Doom—cast into the place where forever there is "weeping, and wailing, and gnashing of"—gums, as Burns has it.

What was the prevalent idea of childhood in a vicinity where this was a school-book, and its author eminent as a theological instructor? For it appears that this Wigglesworth was the same who was eulogized by Cotton Mather in 1710.

Nearly all are ready to ridicule this ancient Calvinism; but many hold an idea which will be looked upon as equally barbarous for our age with Wigglesworth's for his, among those who shall follow us by a century. How many believe now that a child is naturally lost in Adam, and that there is a *necessity* that the child should live on in sin until something shall happen, styled its conversion? Why, it is not proper and evangelical for a child not to be vicious naturally; and presently we shall have it affirmed, that innocence in a child is only a precocious tendency toward the dreadful heresy which denies original sin.

Where doctrines are speculative merely, or where they fall upon rough mature men of the world, who are in little danger of thinking too much on such subjects, we do not care to waste time on theological controversies. But it is where the hard vice-grasp of Calvinism is fastened on the child that our outcry must be heard. For centuries, the Juggernaut Church has been rolled forward on a child's heart. Its books and pietistic dogmas hang about their necks as yokes; its straight-jacket Sabbaths, to which every sparrow, singing on that day as on others, and every merry grasshopper, gives the lie, wither the sweet buds of faith ere they open. I have known mothers, who would turn away a nurse because she would frighten the children with ghost-stories and the like, who will take those children themselves, and string out pictures of the lake of fire and brimstone, of devils, and of God's face all blackened with wrath, compared with which the ghost-stories are a pleasant pastime. I shall not soon forget a story which I mean to tell, because it really occurred. There was a little girl, who was very much restrained and silenced on Sundays, and was given no other dolls to play with than Jacob, and Esau, and David, and Jeremiah, which she had to spell out all day from the Bible. She could not help complaining one day, when she had been forbidden a favorite picture-book: "O, I do wish Sunday was over." "My child, my child," said the pious mother, "it is wicked to speak so; you will not be fit for Heaven if you feel so. Heaven, my child, is an eternal Sabbath." "Well, mother," said the little girl, as if a bright idea had struck her, "don't you think, if I'm a good girl, God will let me go down to hell and play a little while on Saturday afternoons?"

And one, I knew, whose childhood was wholly blotted out, because he felt that he and his brothers, and cousins, and friends, in all their merry-making, were dancing and playing on the very verge of the lake of fire and brimstone, which burneth forever and ever. God was to him a great death's-head, and the very fountains of joy and love were poisoned. It was related some years ago, that there were children, born in the mines near Manchester, England, "who had never seen a flower," and, when it was presented, knew not what it was, nor whence it came. Many poems and speeches resounded through Christendom thereupon. But are there not all around us subterrene pits and labyrinths of doctrine and superstition, where the children toil on drearily and never see the cheerful flowers of faith and joy in life, with which God has strewn the earth? Life free and happy, music and dancing, bloom not for them. One dark pall, the frown of an ever-offended, terrible God, overhangs all. O Dogma, Dogma, what a Moloch thou art, and how many children are sacrificed to thee!

But, if this hard faith paused when it had crushed the *earthly* joys of childhood and scattered its garlands, it could be better tolerated. It goes far deeper, and embitters the springs of faith and morality. How often have we had persons point us to early manifestations of selfishness and injustice in a child, as evidences of inherent depravity? There is no doubt that parents often chastise their own ignorance and folly in the persons of their children. Take the mass of these selfish and naughty children, what have they been taught? Here is item No. 1 in the Westminster Catechism, to be recited from the time of ability to put words together, until it is entirely retained in the memory:

Ques. What is the chief end of man?

Ans. Man's chief end is to glorify God and enjoy him forever.

By this, the child is notified that the object of its existence is to flatter and gratify God's vanity, and its own selfishness. I know that great theological truths may be extracted from these words by mature persons, but they are surrounded by a hard shell of mere cant, and the child's teeth are not yet strong enough to break through the shell and get the kernel. The idea of God therein, is a Being who is soothed and cajoled by flattery and glorification; in return for which, he gives many good things: this being the interpretation placed on another portion of catechetical instruction, by a little boy:

Ques. Why must we love God?

Ans. Because he makes, preserves and blesses us. The little fellow placed the punctuation after preserves, and with a decided smack of the lips, said, "Because he makes preserves,"—he forgot the rest.

A God, such as a child reads of in the Old Hebrew Testament, and hears of from those who do not see that Christ inaugurated a *New* Testament, because the Old would n't answer; a Jehovah awful and angry; sending out avenging, blood-thirsty angels; selfish; jealous of rival deities; exacting; fond of compliments to his magnificence; unjust; who could not forgive the smallest sin, until blood had been shed; such a God, I say, revolutionizes a child's whole moral nature. The inward Life is throttled; and the outward life, we know, is but an outgrowth of a child's idea of God. What is to keep it from climbing by the standard you give it, and being as wrathful, unforgiving, exacting and fond of flattery as its God is made to be?

I do not mean to affix this to any one denomination exclusively. I fear that while we Unitarians have rejected this heartless method in theory, we retain much of it practically. Not all of our churches have realized the full beauty of the Birthright Church—standing up unhesitatingly to a faith in the native purity of childhood, wherever it may lead us; holding the children to be members of the Church by birth; sanctioning their gayeties and pleasures where they are not wrong; and, by the gift of the communion bread and wine, showing them that we are expecting from them also pure and true lives, and that they too have their Christ-childhood to imitate. We have forgotten the full depth of that incident which planted a Church of which children should be esteemed members on earth. Let me read it over to you: "Then were there brought unto him little children, that he should put his hands upon them and pray: and his disciples rebuked them. But Jesus said, Suffer little children, and forbid them not to come unto me; for of such is the Kingdom of Heaven."

Then, although we reject the catechism where it seems to make life a matter of self-seeking, and recommends piety as a good investment, which will bring something handsome at last, I am often pained to see in home-practice, the same old serpent trailing along. Scarcely a day passes without it. The mother whips or scolds her child for what she considers wrong, and gives him a piece of candy for what he does that is right. Henceforth in the child's vocabulary the definitions stand thus: *Bad act.*—Something intimately related to a flogging. *Good act.*—Something having mysterious connection with a sugar-plum. The essential principle of virtue is here lost altogether. Is it impossible to teach a child that you expect him to be good without being paid for it? When you reward one for being honest or truthful, it is as much as to say, "I supposed you to be a rogue and liar, and because you are not, you deserve this." Expect a child or man to be good, and he will try to be so.—And so the mere punishment or scolding inflicted for misbehavior, does not teach the child that a thing is essentially wrong, but only that it leads to serious inconveniences, and is therefore inexpedient. And all this is a vulgar, useless and threadbare method of treatment. Though children should be restrained from being a trouble to others, still, don't call physical restraint, or punishment, moral training.

Thou poor bad child, with mouth full of falsehoods and, perhaps, oaths, others may abuse and dislike thee—I have no heart for that! Who knows how often the vicious youth saw the terrific contrast between the outer show and inner reality, which curses so many homes; the invective changed to compliment when the person at whom it was leveled appeared; the angry brow radiant with smiles at an instant's warning; the secret anger in the chamber,—the kiss in the parlor? You may send the child to Sunday-school, and give him to read the Sermon on the Mount, but you parents are of more importance than Jesus and his discourses in this sphere; and, as Thackeray has said, "in the child's mouth, Mother is another name for God."

"Is it well with the child?" So asked the prophet of the Shunamite woman. She could not speak: her child was dead. How often do we ask the question, and are told, "the child is well!" No! it is not well; it is as dead as the poor widow's. The child has fled, and left in its place a mass of vanity, affectation, and fine clothes. Between catechisms, puritanic Sabbaths, and bad home influences, which should be treated under the head of childrens' diseases, the child (the real child) pined away and left us, leaving us, as before said, the bundle of vanity and fine clothes, which the fond mother still calls her child, and clings to, though it abuses, and disobeys, and hates her! When I think over the amount of ignorance of their nature, the bad influences, the number of catechisms and Sabbaths through which children come, I wonder that every other man I meet is not a scoundrel; and that they should ever come to church is a miracle.

With the reverend Channing, we must place the office of *educator* above that of clergyman, or any other. And there is no problem of so much moment to society at present as, What is the best means of educating the child, and what the best means of elevating the teacher; securing such funds for this office as will command the highest faculties and culture; for it takes nothing less to deal with the child. What a rare combination of qualities does it require to unfold carefully the man from the bud, bringing forth, by due light and warmth, every folded petal of genius or feeling! Any violence or bruising is felt ever after. For the ancients had the true idea of education, as implied in that word, which is from *e* and *duco*—to lead out. Culture is not to fill up the child's mind from without, as if it were a cavity to be heaped full of whatever geographies or languages contain; but it is to unfold what is in it; and for this the world exists—books being but indexes to what is in the world.

The difficulty of the task arises from its extreme delicacy. Teaching, which now we find given to anybody, is the finest of fine arts. It is as if one handled the delicate colors of the butterfly. Nothing, to these children, is trivial or unimportant; all is symbolic and real, even your play with them. As, in their walking, leaping, and antics, they are really learning the laws of gravity, and the qualities of matter which delight or bruise them, so in their joys, waywardnesses, repentances, they are learning the laws of their moral being; and they know much more, generally, than they can give the faintest hint of in words.

We are apt to forget this, the plastic nature of the child, because, in our mature age, we know everything comes to us, as it were, through a strainer, woven of our prejudices, habits, and preferences. We believe what we have a mind to. But the constitution of the child acts not yet by conscious independent exercise of will. It is a part of nature, and acts by instinct or necessity, as water falls or wind blows. And so it must use what it can get; and as a shell-fish will arrest and absorb every atom of sediment, of whatever kind, which floats near it, to form its conch, so is every passing circumstance or word eagerly appropriated by the young. How important, then, that all the circumstances attending the development of the child should be of a high and pure character, so that the mind, body and soul shall come forth in the beautiful chorus of a life high in aim and attainment!

Though we must needs draw the picture of the evil demons which surround the cradle and earlier years with very black lines, let us not be blind to the immense distance we have journeyed beyond Wigglesworth, nor to the wonderful appreciation of the subject of childhood, and the need of a new literature for it, which is altogether the most striking characteristic of this generation. What do our teachers say now? They do not utter the old puritanic abuse of the children. Swedenborg, though seeking to preserve the Calvinism of his age in an introverted mystic way, sees, with the pure eyes of Eve, in each child, a man from the Lord; sees sleeping there so softly, the Titanic passions and powers which may rise to bless or curse the race. "The sphere of innocence," says Swedenborg, "flows into infants, and through them into parents, and affects them. The innocence which flows in is from the Lord, because he is innocence itself." He makes their place in heaven correspondent to the eyes of God. Novalis pauses amid his woes to say:

"Where children are, there is the golden age." Emerson has called the infant the "perpetual Messiah."

Is all this too much? I think not. We sit together in our social life, in a hard shell of conventionality, without a moment of self-forgetfulness, with the bit of ceremony in our mouths; no sign of real life is given by any one, for fear of some one's whispering, "How eccentric!" conversing of weather, crops, and congress. The infant is brought in by accident, and the circle is regenerated in an instant. It cannot speak much, but stupid indeed is that age or sex which cannot read a whole Elizabethan literature in its clear diamond eyes, and hear poetry and music in its prattle. It brings us into the golden age once more.

Is it not the perpetual Messiah? The Christ seemed to think so; for amid the dissensions of his disciples, and their low apprehensions of his Evangel, his whole decision and lesson was to set a young child in their midst, the symbol of innocence and trust. Why should we wonder that the Church of Rome, though crowned with superstition, and clad with a robe of darkness, should have ever had its great and true soul in every generation? Why should we marvel that the earnest St. Austin, the saintly à Kempis, the truthful and gifted Pascal, the heavenly-minded Fenelon, the strong-hearted Luther, were reared in that Church? Throughout its darkest ages, up over the blood on the path it has come; over the lurid fires kindled for dissenters; above the rage of evil-minded cardinals and popes;

above the dark inquisition—there shines on through its history one clear, steady light, which could not fail of its work. It is the holy child. There, carved by ablest hands, painted by devout minds, the child rests on its mother's breast, adored, loved; rebuking all evil passions, all meanness, all falsehood, by the serene innocence of its face, it was indeed the redeemer of the apostate Church. What guilt could be cherished in its presence? Did it not speak to every father, every mother of the little one at home, stirring the holiest fountains of feeling? There it stood, the mother pressing it to her heart, the perpetual Messiah in every Church; silently contradicting all that was false and rotten in the service or sermon. The Church unconsciously bore in her bosom the elements of her own destruction; for in worship of the child, men were led again to simplicity and truthfulness, such as could not co-exist with Jesuitism, or cruelty, or the lust of power.

Again must the holy child be exalted in our churches; and, through gathering about us the child-like spirit, we must see God's spirit moving upon the chaos of society, and bringing forth the verdure of another Eden. "Christine," cried the people, at the death of Gustavus—"Christine shall be our queen!" And the little girl of seven was brought out in the arms of a rugged Norseman, cheerful and happy, and was crowned Queen of Sweden. Happy nation, whose rough soldiers acknowledged the beautiful sway of a child's kind heart to be more than the wisdom of ambitious lords. It did but anticipate the higher day of prophecy, when the rough, warring passions and interests of men shall acknowledge the scepter of innocence and love: the wolf also shall dwell with the lamb within us, and the leopard shall lie down with the kid; and the calf, and the young lion, and the fatling together; and a little child shall lead them.

We must remember, then, as a Church, what an important element we have in our midst; one which we must either, as a Church, ignore as not of God's household, but of Satan's, or else absorb into our organic life. It is our highest duty, perhaps, as a Church, to lead the inborn trust of a child up to Him who implanted it. We should see that the pleasantest associations of life are connected in their minds with our Church; and it will always be a sure test of a church whether the young people love it. We should, as far as is proper, mingle with the gayeties of the children, that we may possess an influence on their graver moments. We should tell them that music was established by the dear Father in Heaven, and also flowers, and May-days. Let them know that it is *He* that has set the young blood to music; and that dancing is a part of their nature, *all* of which *He* has made; that *He* also pre-arranged laughter and fun. And when the Christmas comes around, we should alter the word Kris-Kringle, which they use, into Christ-Kindlein, of which it is a corruption — Christ-Kindlein, or the Christ-Child. Tell them that his birth made the

Christmas; that he loved children, and gives them gifts now by putting it into our hearts to love them, and make them as happy as we can.

To what great importance does the Sunday-school rise! I hate the phrase Sunday-school, because it is associated with much that is silly and morbid in most minds; but I mean a Sunday-school such as we know *may* exist. Not a place for tasks should it be; the children have mental tasks through the week, and we have no right to rob them of their days of rest. In Virginia, where the poor have no means of education, the little Methodist or Baptist Sunday-school, out in the woods, is of wonderful importance, and one child in every twenty learns to read from them; and I have known little girls of ten walk every Sunday five miles for the inestimable privilege. But the ideal Sunday-school would seem to me to be an adaptation of the church to the age of the child. Simple as we may try to be in the pulpit, it is impossible to impress on the children subjects which imply a knowledge and experience which they cannot have. But still every truth enunciated has a corresponding statement, which may reach the child's mind. And I will take it on myself to say, running the risk of all that may be expected of me after it, that it is the duty of a minister to prepare himself as elaborately for discourses to the Sunday-school as to the pews.

Let me also remind the youth of both sexes in this church, that it is not only an important duty to contribute what they can toward the cultivation of these children, but that it is an important privilege and source of culture to themselves. I venture to affirm, that no amount of information can make an intelligent person of one who has never watched and assisted in the unfolding of a human mind: one book, the grandest of all, written by God's pen, lies unknown to such a one. When I go into any Sunday-school, and find it leading a lingering consumptive existence, and find the young, who should be there as pupils or teachers, absent, I say to myself, This church is composed of very pleasant people, no doubt, but they are not up so high yet that they can enter here!

But in our church, with our ideas of human nature, its greatness and destiny, not to have a living intercourse of this kind with the young is unpardonable. Above all, as the center of the school, should we have an excellent library. I know if all the books to be had now were what they used to be, you might well excuse yourselves and children from having anything to do with them. Ah! how well we remember the pious fiction of James, who *would* go playing in the water when his mother forbade it, and was drowned; of George, who went into the street on Sunday, moved and instigated thereunto by the devil, and was logically run over by a coach. O dear! the very memory of what I have suffered in childhood, at the hands of Tract Societies and Sunday-school Unions, makes me shiver; and to this day, I never see any poor little red-riding-hood, who has been waylaid by one of those wolfish books, that I am not irresistibly reminded of the British merchant, who, one day, determined to make an immense outlay of parental affection, and take his two little boys out into the country. Solemnly they marched out, and, when arrived, the affectionate business-man laid down his cane, and seizing either of the youngsters by the collar, said: "Now, boys, I've brought you out here to enjoy yourselves, and if you don't enjoy yourselves pretty quick, you'll catch it, that's all!"

But, thank Heaven, we are no longer necessarily chained to these societies and their books. More than in the Submarine Telegraph, do I see the superiority of this age in the tendency of the highest genius, the world over, to bring its very highest faculties for the entertainment of the children. This was never heard or dreamed of until this generation. We should hail the entrance into this sacred sphere, of such authors as Hans Andersen, the Brothers Grimm and Zschokke in Germany; Thackeray, Dickens, Charles Kingsley, and the Howitts in England; Cranch and Hawthorne in America, as the reddening dawn of a new element in our age—reverence for the child. Of the latter of these, Mr. Hawthorne, as the first of our language who entered this new vein, and the one who has mined it with the best success, we must be more special in our remarks. His are, unquestionably, the best children's books ever written. All his earlier series of tales, "The Twice-told

Tales," "Mosses from an old Manse," "Snow-image, and other Tales," though written for adults, are good enough for children—which is the highest praise that can be given to a book: they may be well placed in the hands of children of fourteen or fifteen years. But those written for children especially, (though I am sorry for him who ever gets too old to enjoy them), "True Stories for Boys and Girls," "Wonder-book," "Tanglewood Tales," are the best expressions of his genius, and entirely free from the somewhat morbid or shaded coloring of the Scarlet Letter and Blithedale Romance. Hawthorne has not forgotten that he was once a child—which so many forget. If it be true, as is written, that no man knoweth the things of a man, save the spirit of man which is in him, even so, we may say, none can know the things of a child but the spirit of a child. It is the old Christian doctrine, that we enter the Kingdom of Heaven through a child-like spirit. He who can bear this spirit into the experience and culture of age, is the true Priest—the rod blossoms in his hand.

Let us then, my brothers, see that we leave not the tender vines unwatered, untended in God's vineyard. Let us look deeply into the eyes of the child, and see that its and our eyes were kindled at the same supernal fire. Woe, woe to those who break the links which bind them to those days when they were so freshly from Heaven, and which these little ones were intended to perpetuate in our minds! May the Church feel that it has a maternal interest in these as *her* children, as well as their parents! And, may the Church, seeing that to them all our faith and hope are soon to be committed, when we shall lie down to rest from life's struggle; that those softly sleeping babes, these playful children, must one day be unsealed from the casket of youth, and rise as genii, standing strongly for God and the Right, or faltering by the way, for our neglect—may the Church, seeing this, gather about them as a granite fortress, fighting their battles against the superstition, error and evil of the world; seeing in each new-born child, a new center of unlimited influence for weal or woe—a new star kindled in the firmament of Humanity; and bowing before the incarnate mystery, feel with the first mother, We have gotten a man from the Lord!

THE BIBLE.

All Scripture is given by inspiration of God, and is profitable for doctrine, for reproof, for correction, for instruction in righteousness.

Now, first of all, I must say that there is no such sentiment as this in the Bible. It was solely in the minds of King James' Translators. If you will examine this passage (2 Tim., 3, 16), in your Bibles, you will find that the word *is*, in the first clause of the sentence, is in italics; which, you know, always means in the Bible, "supplied by the translators." In the supply of this little word, the whole intent of the passage is destroyed. The passage literally translated, without any word *not* in the original, reads, "Every scripture (or writing) *given* by inspiration of God, is profitable,"—and so on.

By it is opened up before us the great Problems of Inspiration, Revelation, Infallibility and Authority. They concern deeply our views of a Book which has had more to do with the life of mankind and the History of the World, than all other books together: a Book which will be proclaimed from ten thousand pulpits this day, as the infallible Word of God, as surely as if the sky had divided and the volume fallen from its heart: a Book, to which has been attached every shade of importance, from that confirmed by the Helvetic Confession of 1675, which made a belief in the inspiration of every vowel point in it, a matter of life and death, through the critical views of modern Germany and England, which, commencing with Luther's rejection of many canonical books, has embraced such churchmen as Coleridge, Arnold, Tholuck and Neander, under the title of rational interpreters, (who believe the Bible in the main true, but by no means infallible,) and a few who have rejected it altogether, as unworthy of confidence.

It requires a sort of animal courage to plunge into this whirl of conflicting views; but there is no question of more importance, especially in this country, where the Bible is so universally accessible; and I have faith that, by mutual frankness and charity, we may attain a reasonable view, which will not obscure, but brighten this "lamp to our feet and light to our path."

In all nations there are what are called the *Sacred Books.* The Turk has his Koran; the Hindoo his Puranas; the Persian his Desatir; the Jew his Hebrew Scriptures; the Christian his Greek Testament. Each of these has an equally implicit faith in the excellence and superior inspiration of his Bible. Walter Scott, when dying, asked for a book: when asked "what book?" he is reported to have said, "What book!

There is but one book." It was a proverb, at one time, that a clergyman should be *homo unius libri*—a man of one book; and people were scandalized by seeing him with other books than the Bible. But this Bible-worship has its strict parallel in the other nations. The Caliph Omar ordered the great Alexandrian Library to be burnt; for, said he, "The value of all books is in the Koran; if true, what they say is in that, if not true, we want them not—burn them!"

The idealization and worship of some outward object, seems to be the first result of the action of the religious sentiment—the infantine grasp of Reverence. This underlies all Idolatry; of which the animating sentiment is good, but the object partial. Idolatry of outward rules comes next; the Fire-worshiper has his sunrise; the Catholic his Church; the Protestant his Bible. The Jew, thinking that God cared only for his nation, felt at liberty to exterminate, mercilessly, all other nations; the Romanist, believing the ark of Noah typified his Church, announces that all outside of it are to be lost; and the Bibliolater excommunicates all who will not fall down and worship the Scriptures. The Trinitarian Coleridge wisely predicted, that the Idolatry of uncivilized nations would be followed by Bibliolatry among the civilized. So the event has proved. Men can scarcely even consider the question of the Bible calmly; and discussion here easily passes into intolerance.

It was one of those enchanted days of early autumn,

when the many-colored vesture of nature, giving the sign of smiling decay, touched the heart to a deeper tone; a fair Sunday, when God's breath filled the earth and sky, and forsook not the reverent heart, that I met a dear old friend and classmate, from whom I had long been separated. We had loved and labored for the same faith once, but now our paths had parted widely. Yet there I saw the same earnest eye—the brow with the same seals of truth and intellect which were the rivets of our former friendship. I cannot forget that walk which made the whole day flit by as a shadow. Thus began our conversation. "I have been thinking (he said) of the death of our poor S., and how it is written, 'It is a fearful thing to fall into the hands of the living God.'"

"Is it possible (I said) that you think he has fallen into worse hands than when he was among his friends on earth? Does God love him less than we?"

"He was unconverted, and I quoted from the Bible."

"But do you not see that you are following Judaism and not Christianity; it may be a fearful thing to fall into the hands of a Jewish Jehovah, but not a Christian Father."

"But 'holy men of old wrote as they were moved by the Spirit.'"

"But this does not say that the *writings* were inspired, but only the good *men*. You must take notice that in the Scriptures the human element is mentioned as fully as the spiritual. 'Holy *men* wrote.' What idea of inspiration do you hold to?"

"The literal authenticity of the word of God."

"So do I, when I can find it. But because a collection of books is made up, neatly arranged and bound in one, does not constitute it the word of God. Now, I undertake to affirm, that *no one believes in the literal authenticity of the Bible.* Do not start, but tell me, if you, for instance, believe that the sun stood still over Ajalon, to await the massacre of the Gibeonites?"

"Of course I am aware (he replied) that the statement that the sun stood still, was founded on the exploded idea that the sun moved round the earth; but I believe that the earth stood still so long."

"To set aside, then, the question, whether this universe paused for a small band of Jewish barbarians to wreak their vengeance on a village of men and women, you admit that the sun's standing still is not exactly the same as the earth's standing still; and that the spirit which moved the writing of that statement, was not quite so wise as Copernicus?"

"If that is what you mean by literal authenticity, I will admit that the Bible is not *verbally* inspired. But I hold to the accuracy of its particular statements."

"By admitting that there may be *verbal* inaccuracies in the Bible, you allow that there is *some* limit to its inspiration. That implies that men must find that limit; for if there be verbal inaccuracies, men must discover them. But that involves the right of our private judgment to criticise. The right to discriminate in one thing includes the right to discriminate in all."

"I agree."

"Then I will proceed to show you how mistaken you are in supposing, that you, or any one who reasons this far, believes in the particular statements; my position, mark you, not being that the reason shall be limited to what any class shall maintain to be alone reasonable, but what all shall acknowledge. It will not do to say, that because this or that is a miracle, the reason will not own it; because it is not conceded by all that a miracle is unreasonable."

My friend expressed his surprise; for it is a common error, that those who discredit the infallible dogma, do it from mere disbelief in God's power to make a revelation, and confirm it by miracles.

"Now, first (I proceeded), there are cases of *direct contradiction*, where you are actually forced to reject one thing in order to believe another of two affirmations. Compare, for example, the accounts given of Judas in St. Matthew and the Acts. Matthew states (27: 3), that Judas repented, brought again the twenty pieces of silver, cast them down, and went and hanged himself; that the chief priests, after consultation, bought a place to bury strangers in with the money, which place was called the "field of blood," because it was purchased with the price of blood. The author of the Acts states, that Judas purchased a field with the reward of his iniquity, and, falling headlong, burst asunder in the midst, and his bowels gushed out, *on which account* the field was called Aceldama, or Field of Blood. Now, unless your mind can entertain such contradictions as that the chief priests could have bought this field, after Judas had died, with the same money which Judas had paid for it before he died; that Judas cast away the money, and bought a field with it also; that Judas could have died in two entirely different ways; that the field was called Aceldama both because Judas died on it, and because the price of Christ's blood purchased it—you cannot believe the 'particular statements' of the Bible without some reservation. Another instance is the account of Paul's conversion, given in two different portions of the same book—the Book of Acts. In 9: 7, we are told, that 'the men which journeyed with Paul stood speechless, hearing a voice, but seeing no man.' In the 22d: 9, Paul himself says, that they saw the light, but heard no voice. It is an exact counter-statement; in one their fear being ascribed to hearing a voice, and seeing nothing; in the other to seeing a light, but hearing nothing."

"I must honestly concede these inconsistencies, since you draw my attention to them," said my friend, "but you will as honestly allow that they are of no special importance to any revelation of truth to mankind."

"Of none, except to show us the possibilities of error in the best of such professed revelations."

"I must still maintain," he continued, "that the

Bible is authentic, in respect of any fact in nature, history, or morals, which affects man."

"Would you regard an error, committed in the very point which a writer started out to establish, as proving the Bible not authentic in that regard?"

"I certainly should."

"Let us, then, examine the account of the deluge. There having been some dispute about the size of Noah's ark, I will agree to put it outside of the largest computation, so as not to have the charge of making it too small. Let it be 500 by 100 feet in size: it would be all one to my point if it were twenty times that size. Now, it is known that there have always been on earth more than 150,000 species of animals. Of each species, Noah is said to have taken a pair of the unclean (under Jewish laws) and seven pairs of the clean. This would amount to having in an ark of 500 by 100 feet about five or six hundred thousand animals, of the largest as well as smallest sizes. With these animals, which could not be gathered in an ark twice the size of Cincinnati, with food enough to sustain them for the hundred and fifty days in which, it is stated, the waters prevailed, with one window only, Noah and his family were shut up. Mind you, this does not rest on the idea that this is impossible because supernatural; there is no intimation that there was anything supernatural. The ark was said to have been made so large in order to admit all the different animals of which the writer, who was no Cuvier, knew; that they were not fed by miracle, is plain, from the distinct assertion that enough food was taken for them all. Then what are we to think of this account of the deluge. 'All the high hills that were under the whole heaven were covered. Fifteen cubits upward did the waters prevail, and the mountains were covered.' It is stated, in the Bible, that this water came in the natural way, by rain, and from the fountains of the great deep, which were broken up; and we are, therefore, forbidden to think that it was added from without the natural elements, which God caused to break forth. Now, it is very easy to demonstrate, that all the water in the earth itself would not be able, if it covered the earth from the line of circumference upward, to reach to the tops of the highest mountains on the planet, or even the small hills. All the water which could come, in the way stated in the Bible, from the seas and rain, would not cover the surface of the earth higher than some houses. Remember—we must, if we believe the Bible, believe its assertions as much *as to the way* in which it is done as to the main event; and are not at liberty to suppose a miracle where the Bible declares there was none."

"I must confess (said my friend,) that I cannot see that it would be of importance, to have a revelation of scientific accuracy. But, will you not agree with me, that in all that bears upon the *moral duties* of man and his relation with God, this book is authoritative?"

"I must really qualify my words before I can assent

to that. I should not like to give the Bible to a child with any intimation that its moral standard was to be always revered. I would not like to place before the child King David, as a man after God's heart, as he is called, for, setting aside his conduct to Uriah, of which he repented, does this, from the 137th Psalm, read like the writing of a 'man after God's heart?' 'Oh Daughter of Babylon, who art to be destroyed, happy shall he be who rewardeth thee as thou hast served us! Happy shall he be that taketh and dasheth thy little ones against the stones!' Nor should I be willing to give to children, who have mothers and fathers, the following misanthropic saying of a jaded sensualist, as the true inspiration of the wisest of men. (Ecc., 7: 27.) 'Behold this have I found, saith the preacher, counting one by one, to find out the account; which yet my soul seeketh, but I find not: one (good) man among a thousand have I found; but a (good) woman among all those have I not found.' The youth then, are to have it on the authority of the Word of God, that there is not more than one man to a thousand who may be trusted, and not one woman! And what idea is the following to give concerning the nature of the human soul? (Ib. 3: 18) 'I said in mine heart concerning the estate of the sons of men, that God might manifest them, and that they might see that they themselves are beasts; for that which befalleth the sons of men, befalleth beasts; even one thing befalleth them; as the one dieth, so dieth the other; yea, they have all one breath; so that a man hath no pre-eminence above a beast; for all is vanity. All go unto one place; all are of the dust, and all turn to dust again.' Very natural speculations for King Solomon in the midst of his seven hundred wives, princesses, and three hundred concubines; but not quite good enough, to place in the hands of those whom we desire to believe that there *is* a difference between a man and a beast! And you, my friend, no more than I, can believe in the unqualified moral authenticity of a book, which represents a just God as hardening Pharaoh's heart, and then punishing him and all Egypt for the hardness of one man, which he had himself caused in order to make a display of his power; or, as commanding Moses and Aaron to tell Pharaoh a deliberate falsehood, saying that Israel was only going a little way into the wilderness to sacrifice to their God, when they really designed running off entirely; or as commending Jael, who, for a political end, betrayed Sisera, her husband's friend, into his tent, and while he was asleep, drove a spike through his head!"

My friend was silent, and we soon parted; I to urge these facts upon all before whom I am called, in God's providence, to stand; he to find, I trust, a sunnier faith than that with which I found him clogged.

But now it is asked, "Do you then reject the Bible altogether?" NO.

There is a strange illusion abroad, that the Bible is a unit; that if you touch one stone in this nicely-wrought arch, all the rest will fall to the ground. There never was a greater blunder: of all books on the face of the earth, there is none of such variety of dates, authenticity, subjects. Few can tell why they believe any of them authentic; but it is a familiar thing to students of the Bible, that it was but by a few votes of fallible men, that we have not now several books of the Old and New Testaments, which have been decided to be apocryphal; and that only by a few human votes, were several of those still preserved retained. The Church has always been wavering as to what was Bible, and what was not; and as to who wrote various books. It is common to hear of the Books of Moses,—yet you cannot suppose that Moses wrote the Pentateuch, unless you suppose that he was capable of giving a minute account of his own death and ceremonies of burial. It is proved, by orthodox critics entirely, that Paul did not write the Epistle to the Hebrews, and some other things ascribed to him. Such a book calls for great discrimination.

It is utter absurdity to say, that one who rejects any portion of it, must reject all. Profound logic! Because in a garden I gather for food potatoes and peas, I must take along also, nightshade and artichokes! Because some superstitions, which no child would now own, are found in Plato and Lord Bacon, therefore all they wrote is superstition! This is the reasoning which would say, that because we will not believe everything in the Bible, we must reject it; and have no business with preaching from it and commending it.

We affirm that our common sense, our moral sense, our ability to investigate, are given us *for the purpose* of our distinguishing what is credible, what incredible, what healthful, what hurtful to the mind and soul; as we have faculties to distinguish between vegetables which are good food, and those which are poisons.

Have you ever thought what a curse an infallible Bible would be to the world?

Let us suppose for a moment that the fruits of the world, and all the products which support the race, should come henceforth without labor, and the law no longer hold, "In the sweat of thy brow shalt thou eat bread." What would become of the physical development of mankind, which is known to depend on labor? It is manifest that man would dwindle into feebleness in a few generations, and presently become extinct. How would it be with the intellect? Suppose it should henceforth be the plan of school-teachers, after giving children their various problems, to go around and give each solution and answer, so that there should be no need for any child to make any intellectual effort. It is plain that education is at an end; that mental powers, dependent, like the body, on labor, must lose their vigor. Yet this spontaneity of harvests and donations of unearned knowledge are parallel to the gift of a revelation to the soul. If Genesis gives us the true history of creation, and the laws of nature, they are not left to be discovered, of course. What, then, is left to develop such men as Leibnitz and Agassiz? Does not the existence of such men *presuppose* that things *are not* revealed? What mental strength can be derived from laws unfolded more than physical from harvests unlabored? Let us carry this consistently into the moral and spiritual life; for there is a science of the soul also, and laws surrounding it; and we affirm that, as fruits without labor would be physical degeneracy, knowledge without thought and invention ultimate idiocy, so a revelation of moral and spiritual truths, without exercise of the soul to attain them, would be moral and spiritual weakness and vastation. Hence a book which should be acknowledged, without test, a revelation of these things, superseding the activity of the spiritual faculties, would be the bane, not the blessing, of mankind.

Any Protestant can see this principle acting in Romanism. There a person goes to the confessional; the priest is his conscience to tell him right or wrong. The soul is not required to act on its own sin, but to obey blindly the verdict of the priest. It is easy to see that, under such treatment, the conscience rusts and perishes by disuse, as fishes in caves, where there is no light to exercise the nerves of vision, have no eyes. This fact easily explains to a Protestant the low mental and moral condition of Catholic countries. Yet how does this differ essentially from having the action of the conscience superseded by a set of written texts and rules? In one case, it is priest; in another, book; in neither, the soul.

The error of expecting or believing in an infallible book-revelation, arises from the old heathenism, that God *needs something* of man for his glory or happiness. Many unconsciously imagine that God has a book or creed in the world, which he very much needs men should believe, and if they do not, will be insulted and angry. But when we know that all is for the culture and elevation of man, and that this implicit reliance on an external authority disparages the self-reliance and energy within which are the conditions of strength, the matter is plain.

Another view to be taken is, that this so-called infallible revelation comes through human language. Language is fallible, being the outgrowth of man. How can an infallible revelation come through a fallible medium, retaining its infallibility? That it does not, is shown by the fact that a simple text often strikes ten men in ten different ways. Christ in the Bible says plainly, My Father is greater than I. The obvious conclusion of all would be, that God was greater than Christ. But the teachers come in and say, that this means that the divine was greater in him than his earthly nature, and give other indirect meanings. Well; but do they not show in that explanation, that the Bible needs their aid to rescue it from the imperfections of language? So, by this showing, it would follow that the Romanists are right in saying, that an infallible book renders an infallible interpreter necessary, which they furnish in an infallible Church. What is the use of an infallible revelation, if, because of the imperfections of men and language, one understands one thing from a text, and another the opposite, as is the case with Unitarians and Trinitarians in regard to the simple saying of Christ, "My Father is greater than I?"

Having then inquired, What the Bible *is not*, let us see in what sense *it is* a revelation. For we *do* believe it to be a revelation in the highest sense—a revelation by reason of its errors and immoralities no less than by its truths. I know there are some who are ready to ask, If the soul learns all from within, what use can it have for any book or external influence? It is enough to reply to these, that the soul needs revelation from without *because* it has revelation within. The very *want* of a revelation, is itself a revelation. The rain is not more refreshing to any flower than the water-lily, though it is, and *because* it is surrounded by water. Euclid is a mathematical revelation to the youth, only because the youth has a mathematical faculty. But let us trace the sources of revelation.

From the beautiful groves of Arezzo, Michael Angelo wrote thus to his friend Vasari: "Here I am fed with angel's food. The thunder speaks to my ear with the voice of ages; the winds come rushing with Almighty power. They talk of nature, and what is nature but the Spirit of God, filling man with inspiration?"

Ah! there is where inspiration begins. Before this fair and wonderful apparition, called Nature, as a bird sings its joy, the great soul utters itself in prophecy and revelation. When natural objects and laws are interpreted into meaning for the Spirit, that is truth, and truth is always divine. Wherever truth is, God is. Swedenborg saw that whenever some angels announced a truth, a twig which they held in their hands blossomed. The first race of prophets is the flowers and stars, which, through any wise and pure soul, blossom to truths far grander than any flowers or stars.

But if mere nature be inspiration to her true lovers and interpreters, how much more any insight into that being in whom all nature culminates—*Man;* for surely man is *the meant* of nature—all the gradations of form, from lowest plants to highest animals, being but hints and prophecies of his advent. In him, all the excellencies of other beings were concentrated. To him, as their king, all owe homage.

Well, now, what if there be a book which truly records the development and destiny of this wonderful being—a book which gives faithful history of the credulities, speculations, errors, follies of his race's infancy and boyhood; of the rising of higher stars of knowledge and insight, through slow experiences of ages; of the night and gray twilight of this being dissolving into the magnificent dawn of a world's holy religion? Would not that be a revelation of man? and because man is God's image, his nature God's work, must it not be God's revelation also? Suppose to a geologist the earth should suddenly become transparent; every fossil accessible; the gradations of form—from the central rocks up to the crust, open to his examination—would that not be a revelation, or "a drawing back of the vail" from the earth? But man also has a geology. In any true biography of the race, we see successive strata of life; here also are fossil superstitions and ideas as in the earth are saurian and dactyl. And though, as the old monsters are extinct, demanding for their existence primitive stages of the world, many of the old thoughts and statements imbedded in Old Testament sandstone are extinct, yet do they reveal human development spiritually, as fossils reveal the development of the animal creation materially. You will see readily, that the difficulty men have with the Bible *versus* Science and Morality, arises from an attempt to make it out a direct supernatural revelation from God; it being natural enough for the human mind, in its early days, to imagine the sky to be a *firmament*, or firm, solid arch, but incredible that God should have called it so. Thus you see we are not troubled with those difficulties. What we find in the Bible, which is not strictly true or moral, we take as the best evidence of the genuineness of the book. If not true to science, it is true to human nature. A book brought up to the standard of a French academy in its scientific accuracy, or to transcendental ethics in its moral rules, would smack of some secret council of modern times.

Suppose a correct theory of the stratification of the earth, or a catalogue of animal genera and species, were found in Genesis, who would believe it to have been written in the age it professes? But there, with all its imperfections, superstitions, immoralities united to so much that is divine, is so exact a counterpart of man as he is, that we know it is true; and it is as much a revelation in its blunders as in its truths.

Take the book; examine its language, ideas, structure, and see if it does not bear the impress of man from childhood to maturity. Its account of a six days creation, after which, God was fatigued and must rest; the firmament, which was a solid wall, dividing the waters in the earth from the waters above it, so that when it rained the windows of Heaven are supposed to be opened to let the water through; are not these the speculations of children? Then the dire judgments of Jehovah, Egyptian plagues, the swallowing of Pharaoh and his host in the Red Sea, the Deluge; are they not the prodigies of the nursery of the race?

But the childhood passes, and we have the earnest action of political and social life. The celebration, not of God's prodigies, but of the achievements of men, and the splendor of kings. Here is a race's self-reliant youth. Then earnest life and experience distil their deeper meanings. Manhood rises in prophecy. And now on, profounder, profounder, runs the ever-widening human spirit; through great action, lofty prophecy, elevated hymns; until the soul of a people, striking

Heaven with its sublime front, gathering the experience and insight of foregone ages,—as the aloe its accumulated strength of ninety-nine years for its century-blossom—bursts forth into that Evangel which redeems the World!

The Bible of a nation, is all which expresses the soul of that nation. Thus we revere the Bible of the Hebrews, because of its superior naturalness and humanity. The Human soul everywhere, in all ages, finds its wants, satisfactions, sympathies, consolations, there, because the human soul wrote it. If I had not written the Bible, I could not find my emotions so faithfully recorded there; that is, it was written by that common heart of mankind to which we are all inlets. So, also, there is not an error or crime recorded there, but flows directly from the nature we all partake; thus making it as well the "sword of the spirit," as a "lamp unto our feet." It is indeed the Book of Books, because the most faithful epitome of Man.

And this simple rule applies, not only to the Books of Narrative, but to those of prophecy, poetry, and the divine oracles of Christianity. When we remember that the human soul is a divine being, wandering through the world gathering forces for a higher life, how sacred become her traces and footprints! And in this sacred volume, we believe may be found, nature new-created and transfigured through the Soul! Only from its depths can prophecy come; for the human soul is the one thing alone which we can think of as reaching God. Prophecy and vision are not then supernatural, but the very height of the *natural*. It is the flower of actual life. "Art thou a soothsayer, good Mother?" said Apelles to Zara. "Who," she cried, "who that has lived to see the raven hair turn to snow; who that has watched the sapling as it grew into the sturdy oak, and has beheld generation after generation swept away; who that has seen all this and yet stands blasted and alone, is not a soothsayer? Aye, young master, age and sorrow have the gift of reading the future by the past."

In nature everything becomes sacred and beautiful when it ceases to be mere outwardness, and becomes knowledge. Serpents and other reptiles, and insects are often loathsome in themselves, but not so when a naturalist is tracing from them God's idea in creation. So Egypt, the Wilderness, Babylon, Jerusalem, are records of crime and error, often of the most disgusting kind; yet from those poisonous roots grew the fairest blossoms of prophecy, and fruits of Christianity.

All experience is really Revelation. How would it be if every one now born should not be able to profit by the laws and facts which have been discovered by those who lived before him? Ages have gone to acquire the laws of Gravitation and Electricity, the axioms of matter, the properties of fire, water, poisons. Now, unless these were revelation to the next generation, each one can only learn these things by being burned, drowned or poisoned in turn. Thus life tried by the

Hebrew people through manifold experiences has been expressed in the Bible. The circumstances are past, and we cannot undergo them ourselves; but they are reproduced here as truth, which is always alive. The more we live and feel, think and act, the more do we discover *how* true is this Book. In it every age of the world brings a contribution to my fireside. I may bear Egypt's yoke and Israel's freedom; the Wilderness, its trials and joys; and blessed Palestine in my own private heart. Is it not thus alone we can live and be nourished by life? Men must live by bread; bread, planted, growing, harvested, kneaded, baked. Dust enough there is unsown, but he cannot eat it; yet that which he does eat is but dust passed from field to oven. So, to his mind, what is mere Nature but dust? But when Nature, overcome by human force and mind, yields experiences of life; and these yield maxims of prudence, wisdom, thought, prophecies, psalms, holy visions; then may the spirit be nourished by it, as the body by bread which was last year's dust. But we must bear in mind, that it is only revelation so far as the soul is able to appropriate it by life and experience. A traveler may tell us of delicious and luxuriant fruits in the tropics, but they are not so good to us as the homeliest fare we really have. It is even so with your maxims, texts, morals; they are idle abstractions, except so far as the life is up to grasping them. The writing must be read in the same spirit which wrote it, and revelation commence in the individual soul, as it commenced in the brain and heart of Isaiah or Paul.

I fear not then for the Bible. Let it be cast forth to the severest tests of Time and Criticism ; let the clearest of the sunbeams play around it. I hate to hear persons express fear that it can be injured by such investigations. Who dares say that any truth can die? Truth is everywhere sealed with the power and immortality of God. And were every sentence in the Bible proved false except one, that one would not be disparaged an iota, but would survive the wreck of all the rest.

Let us not insult God's dominion over the world by any timidity. Least of all can we fear that the Bible shall lose its true authority. More and more as unwise claims are stricken down, and foolish superstitions concerning it fall, it brightens to a value which the Bibliolater, afraid to prove it, can never know. Too long has it been associated with the best that is in every man ; too long the companion of affliction, the solace of toil, the help of faith, for it ever to fail of its divine mission. Scholars may quote Plato in studies, but the hearts of millions shall quote this Book at their daily toil, and draw strength from its inspiration, as the meadow draws it from the brook. Ah no, I cannot for a moment contemplate such a thing as its loss! I have heard of a Fair Island which had long gladdened the sea as a gem ; where voyagers had been wont to pause for its beauty and refreshing fruits and fountains,—

suddenly sinking beneath the waves. But what were that to the loss of this sacred record of Man, and God's dealings with him; to the sinking of this Fair Island, whereon millions of life's weary, tempest-tost voyagers have found repose and comfort? Be not anxious, friends, more than you are anxious for the sun lest it should fail,—lest the true authority of this Bible should be impaired: embalmed in the immortal heart of man, sealed by the Eternal Spirit, its Truth must live as long as these shall live.

MIGNON.

Seek.

Most beautiful among the creations of Goethe is Mignon, the child. Born of a noble family in Italy, in the midst of every luxury and refinement, she was stolen by a band of vagabond actors, and reared in contact with coarseness and harsh treatment. Though stolen at an age to which memory can only recur with twilight indistinctness, her shrinking temperament warned her that the cold German airs were not native with her; her loneliness among her gay companions attested that she was not born with them; and in her mind, there ever floated a cherished, though vague, vision of the beautiful skies, luxuriant gardens, and superb halls and ornaments of her southern home. She yearned for something, she knew not what; but a subtle instinct guided her heart southward. Of those whom she chanced to meet, she would ask if they were going north or south; and if they said the latter, her eyes would light up with unwonted hope, and she would ask them to take her with them—she was so cold there. The child met her first and only friend,

Wilhelm; he cared for her, and soothed her, and she came to worship him. It was when he was sitting alone, that he heard the sound of music, and Mignon entered with her cithern, and sang, with impassioned voice, the finest lyric of modern times, in which all her dreams of home and her vague longings concentrated.

"Knowst thou the land where the citrons bloom,
And the orange lights up the leafy gloom;
A gentle wind from deep blue heaven blows—
The myrtle thick, and high the laurel grows?
Knowst thou it then?
'Tis there! 'tis there!
O, my true loved one, thou with me must go!"

Poor Mignon! she never reached her Italian home; but, while yet a child, she was taken to a fairer home, a sunnier sky, a tenderer father, where the flowers never fade, and love never fails, and none could snatch her away.

Margaret Fuller has called Mignon the type of lyric poetry. She would seem rather the type of all that mysterious yearning, striving thing within us, which we call *the soul*. For is she not God's child—born of his heart, and in his beautiful halls? Surely, "heaven lies about us in our infancy;" and there too are garlands of innocence, and dreams of beauty. What though the poor child is out here among the vagabond passions and follies of life? What though they have borne her away into contact with coarse natures, and she must lead a shrinking life amid the chilling airs of evil?

In secret, she still pines for her first sweet innocent home; she weeps and prays for a hand which shall lead her there. And when we come close to the human heart of any one, let us listen well, and we shall hear the chords swept by an unseen hand, and the music, now "querulously high, now softly, sadly low," of a heart yearning for its Father's house—the land where the fair fruits of the spirit bloom.

I know it is not always so; that there are some whom these dreams and longings for the higher, purer life seem to have deserted; whom Swedenborg appears to have indicated when he spoke of some spirits which he saw in hell, but who were very happy there, and thought they were in heaven. Alas! that were the saddest of all hells. I must think the philosopher was mistaken, and that though there are many who are so deeply absorbed in the merely earthly life, as to be generally forgetful of the spiritual, yet the vision will urge itself vividly, at times, on all, and the home-woe cling to the hardest heart. If there had been some of the Calvinistic film taken from the eyes of Swedenborg, he would have seen, hovering amidst these spirits so contented with their hell, by which is meant the mere physical social life, which so many lead apart from anything higher, another spirit. It is the spirit of DOUBT. Ever and anon she stoops and whispers to one and another: Are dust and ashes fit to make the treasure of a divine soul? . . . . Your neighbor had all these things for which you give up everything; he had wealth, and family, and position; but he sleeps under the sod, and they benefit him not. . . . Are you not ashamed to see how few aims you have in life, which the worm or mole burrowing the clod has not in common with you? They and you seek only comfort, and a supply.

Thus, gliding about, whispers the questioning spirit. There is no man who does not sometimes hear that voice. Then patiently she waits to see if the doubt grow deeper—if some inquiring eye shall be turned to her; and when it is, she has but one word to whisper in the ear; that word is SEEK.

No, no! the soul, in a hell of mere earthliness, can never entirely persuade itself that it is in heaven. And even from the midst of what seems absolute spiritual destitution, when nakedness and starvation have done their utmost, when this spirit has whispered her doubt, and said to the soul *seek*, the poor prodigal catches a glimpse of his awful poverty of spirit, and cries: "I will arise, and go to my Father."

Seek—yes, I must seek; but *what?* Some would say *Regeneration* — some, *Christ* — some, *Culture*. Men have always a disposition to take humanity in the lump, and ask, as one would of a marble-quarry or guano, "What is it good for?" A friend who has recently been in England, and met often with her best man, Carlyle, told me an anecdote of him, which struck me as satisfactory. A fine London gentleman, who wished to know the author, more perhaps from curiosity than anything else, came over from London, and went up toward Carlyle's house. He met him in the street before he got there. "Well, Mr. Carlyle," he said, "I've come into your faith, that every man ought to be set to work, and kept at it; but what now shall a man work at?" "Ah!" was the rough answer, "you're a great fool, to come out here in the rain and mud, and ask a man what ye're to do, when it's what you were put into the world to find out with your heart's blood."

It was God's truth for all its bluntness. What are you to believe amid the clamor of swarming creeds? What, when your mind has plied all mysteries with fervor, honesty, and valor, you shall find to be your own special creed—not the Episcopalian, nor Presbyterian, nor Unitarian creed, but *your own*. Attempt not to climb into the kingdom but by your own door. Pray not the prayers of others, but heed him who said, Enter into *thy* closet. What are you to do in the world? What thy hand shall find that it *can* do, when every sinew aches for its work; when the heart holds itself full under the light of God, as the wool is spread under the bleaching sun—then what it tells thee, obey. What the mind shall seek, or the heart or the hand shall seek, that is the very problem given thy life to solve; the thing for which thy heart's blood is to be paid: seeking alone shall lead thee to it. Christ said: "Seek and ye shall find,"—not "find and ye shall seek."

And thou, O Seeker! who hast heard in aspiring,

growing nature, or the aspiring striving soul, the voice which cries, Seek, and art ready to seek the best and highest life and knowledge which the universe can give, take courage; the path of search is not through the musty volumes of theologians, nor through questions of incarnation and hypostasis, nor through the catacombs of the dead, and fleshless ideas and institutions of the past; but the way is simple and plain before thee; and the light of a few strong instincts, such as God has lodged in every human heart, will shed all clearness that is needed.

First, *seek truthfully*. He who plans at the start, that he will arrive at a certain foregone conclusion, or that there is any conclusion which he is resolved *not* to arrive at, hath a falsehood in his heart. He is no true knight of the seekers; let him give up his sword, and stand aside. Such a man is fonder of himself than the truth, and would flare his conceited little taper in the face of the very sun. The strong man is he who does not adopt ideas, and shape them to the prejudices of himself and those around him; but with the hemlock or the cross in sight, humbles himself before the truth of things, and becomes its faithful mouth-piece; stating not what he or others would have to be so, but what really *is* so. Nature is very obstinate, and shuts down her shell, like a turtle, when you try to force her; and so is it with all truth. I have no faith that a man will fathom any question to any good depth, who fears his plummet will go too far, or fears any conclusion however startling. *Perfect truth*—that is his only line. "But so you shall be led to doubt." Is not a true doubt better than a rotten, false show of belief or certainty? Is it immortality, or God, or custom, or society, that seeking brings into doubt? Let us openly say, "I doubt," if that is the truth of the moment; and when a clearer moment comes, we may say, "I see how it is." That conviction which has never been doubted, is not to be trusted for an instant; even your faith that there is a God is worthless, if never cross-questioned; for we rely upon the solid earth, remembering that there is nothing solid which was not once fluid, and that nothing is certain which has not been doubted and tried.

Then, *seek bravely*. Spiritual, like other fortune, favors the brave; and as Frederick the Great said, "Providence is on the side of the best battalions." Many springs of life, full of health and greatness, gush on unvisited, because men fear to tear away some old dead brambles, sanctified by Church or State, which close all the paths to it. A devotion to absolute justice; what a grand life it opens up in the soul! what strength for the heart is in those waters! But some institution bestrides the way, and men skulk off, and never know justice. Free thought; what inspiration is in it! The naked tree of winter, lifting up its dead arms to the sky, is not more ennobled when, flooded with summer sap, it climbs to a soul in flower and fruit, than the ordinary man is when he resolves to think for himself—to be free from all the trammels of priests and politicians, and put forth, as fruit, his *own* faith and his *own* life; yet society closes up the path to that fountain, and bids you yield the right to think and speak freely, and of yourself, on pain of being called eccentric, or infidel, or fanatical, or mad. Yet is it ever true, as Mohammed said, that "Paradise is under the shadow of swords," and the depths of the heart will echo on with the poet's voice: "O friend! never strike sail to a fear. Come into port greatly, or sail with God the seas. Not in vain you live, for every passing eye is cheered and refined by the vision."

Lastly, *seek earnestly;* and here, alas! is the real point of failure. Man is a creature of motives; hunger and thirst, cold and heat, are comprehensible to all; but the hunger and thirst after righteousness, of which Jesus spoke, are not so comprehensible; for this reason the earth glitters with granite and marble cities, and is clothed with purple and gold; but souls of granite strength, and the white raiments of purity, are more rare, because the senses addressed by these are not generally strong enough to be roused to their objects, as the senses of the body to theirs. The worshipers of the vailed Isis affirm that the chosen incense of their goddess is scentless to all but her true worshipers. It depends on the nature of each of us, its coarseness or fineness of fiber, whether we can be enkindled to a passion for truth, and an enthusiasm for virtue and rectitude. Until a man can come to a kind of scorn of his earthly routine of life, and asks himself, "Am I, an immortal being, to be only a maggot among maggots, striving only to be a little larger and more well-fed than the rest among which I roll along?" he cannot glow with that divine earnestness which leads to the highest truth and beauty; which is to him as the warmer ray, which changes the grub to the beautiful fly with burnished wing. O, what might not men do, if they were only in earnest! Now, see how it is: our moral sentiments, our faith, our religion, are ever yielding, yielding, yielding—never maintaining their ground; pinioned and disabled by the swarm of lilliputian interests, prejudices, and fears which oppose them. Dear brothers, how is this? Is Satan, then, really stronger than God? Cannot God make hearts stout and strong as well as the devil? Why must we be content to see evil uppermost all the time? Why must religion remain, through our timidity, a nightmare of the soul, instead of its glorious dawn?

It is because inspired and enlightened minds and hearts are basely unfaithful; and truths, as glorious as God—truths which fill full, in grand chorus, all the pipes of the universe—fall upon our dull eyes and ears like some election gossip. To be earnest, is to be great. How arid is that desert sand, hot in the sun—the serpents creep over it, and the wolves stretch them on it. But see the rising sirrocco! now it fills and swells it, and lo! the desert sand stands in grand pillars against the heavens, and all things that live and grow, bow and bend before its terror and force! And what else is our poor human dust; lying and barren under the trail of the meanest motives, trodden by the beasts of low passions and cares, until some earnest love of high and noble principles, some superb leap toward the highest expands and inspires us, and the poor dust rises to heaven, and man becomes the awful hand of God, stretching his rod or scepter over the world!

I know the doubt that makes men falter; I have heard that low-toned whisper of the senses which says, "Sugar is sweet, and music, and dancing, and wine make glad the heart, but what know we of virtue and heroism; we cannot taste nor handle them, and only see that their devotees are often in trouble."

It *is* the crowning glory of the Christian virtue that it cannot be bought; here differs the soul from sense: the one acts for private ends, the other without, and often to the detriment of private ends. But its rewards though slow and hidden, are sure and beautiful. Not knowing what you shall find, you must seek; yet the promise remains, Seek, and thou shalt find.

Listen to the story of the old man and his sons. As he was drawing near the closing moment of his life, he said to them, "My sons, all that I have to leave you is hidden away in the field,"—and he died without being able to tell them the spot where the treasure was buried. Then forth went the sons and plowed the field, turning up every clod; but they found no treasures. They planted it that year, and, when the crop was taken in, they dug again for the money, but could not find it, and planted again. When some years had passed thus, a thought struck the eldest of the brothers, and, calling the others, he said, " My brothers; year after year since our father's death we have broken up the field to find the money of which he spoke: we have not, it is true, discovered any bag of gold, but we have worked well and are strong and healthy, and our acres have yielded us a fair income each year. It is my belief that this health and fair income of our labor are the treasures which our father said were hidden in that field." And with him the others agreed.

Ever does the Father leave his children the inheritance, dropping but the one word, *Seek.* Ever do His faithful children cast in the plow and tend every clod to find the golden treasures; and in the very health and strength of soul which flow from the seeking for Truth; in the priceless harvest which grows from the earnestness, the sincerity, the valor which are involved in its pursuit, the endless wealth which the Father bequeaths us is revealed. All around us it lies infolded in nature, in the world of men, and women, and children; in every mystery; in duties, perplexities, temptations, cares; the wonderful alchemy of a seeking spirit touches any of them, and they become gold.

Expand thy heart, O Christian, until it embrace the swarming world! Be embraced, fair Universe; this kiss to all that is; ye bring me bags of gold from my Father, and letters written and signed by him. I will not let any of you escape until I have searched and found your secret, that for which you exist!

For Christianity is seeking—"extraordinary generous seeking." Not from one flowing down with the current and gathering into his shell the sediment that happened to pass, came these life-giving words which uplift the soul as on eagle's wings. See that eager child's face turned up to the doctors in the Temple in anxious questioning! See that youth walking alone in the wilderness of Judea, seeking the secret of nature in tree, and mountain, and the stars! See the man, fasting and lonely seeking in the fierce crucible of Temptation the strength of his godlike soul! Ah that face, look at it! Does it hint of a quiet fireside and slippers; of content and luxury; of a well-conditioned life which ignores all mysteries, all that cannot be felt or seen?

Surely no; but, as we gaze on that restless eye, on that heaven-searching face, we almost look to see the shoulders strike forth in pure white wings, aching for higher, holier spheres, as the only natural complement of such a life and effort. Men watched him as he rose; straining eyes forgot all but him, who, before the gazing world, was changing on from man to angel, from angel to god; but, as he rises above the earth until he is lost to sight, one word falls back to us, as it were the blessed curse of Ahasuerus, cutting off all rest save that which may be found in endless aspiration toward the realm where he has gone. The voice cries, *Seek!*

O man, wilt thou not seek? Ever is there a higher and holier, and wilt thou still give thy heart to the mixed and lower?

This voice came to us as we wandered in the wood—my heart and I—alone. My heart first heard and spoke of the Christ, the Ideal Seeker, and would feign have me follow; had even wept that I was so little kindled to seek.

Hush, my heart! Why must I be forever troubled with discontent and doubt of my life? Let me live my life in quiet! Why lead me to dreams of virtue, and purity, and truth, which I have seen so vaguely? Why cannot I rest and enjoy with the throng? Sad and weary enough now, I am, with following after your beautiful Christ; I must rest: Cease, my heart, to persuade, and let us hope for better things in some other planet, where the current shall not be too strong for us.

Then my heart spake between her imploring sobs: Do not, O do not rest here,—thou who hast been given a vision of the land of a pure knowledge, where the soul comes to the flower of a divine life; where that clod men call human life is turned to violets and roses. 'T is there! 'T is there! O my true loved one, thou with me must go!

But why, my heart, should I leave the seen for the unseen? Is not earth full of beauty and love? Seest thou not the path thou wouldst urge is lonely? There are few who seek these things. Dost hear, in the distance, the joy and music of those who throng the avenues of compliant life? Why follow this phantom called Virtue?

Then my heart cried, Ask this vine why it crept toward this tree rather than where there was no tree? Ask the imprisoned flower why it grows toward the smallest beam of light? Ask the needle why it ever trembles toward the north-star? 'Tis the very nature and essence of a soul to seek endlessly the best. In this Gethsemane of the world, while others, with heavy eyelids, cannot watch one hour but sleep, she, the soul, ever wakeful, goes apart to pray. Canst thou not, with it, watch one hour!

Then I answered not. My heart spake on.

Is not the soul God's child? Is there wonder she should seek her Father's face?

Then her tone deepened, as if a more awful voice had spoken, and I only heard, "When thou saidst unto me, Seek thou my face, my heart said, Thy face, Lord, will I seek."

Then I held out no longer. I turned overcome. There heart and hand took the eternal oath: Yes, in God's name, we will seek forever; we will endure all; will be scorned or hated; will leave father, mother, and all dearest ties, and will SEEK; and wherever and whenever we fall, my heart and I, I know that it shall be with hands and eyes stretched out toward the everlasting summits.

Brother, sister! you whom I love more than you may ever think; you to whom I shall never again appeal—

suffer me to leave in your hearts one word — *Seek*. Seek higher realms of knowledge and faith. Amid all the allurements of life—amid the terrible griping persuasions to selfishness and dapperness, which are stronger in this city than elsewhere—may your heart never forget my parting word; may you never be content, but ever seeking.

And now I am content. I leave it there. It is not so much whether the real voice of our church here be vocal or silent—I know that the standard, where I leave it, is for Truth, Justice, Humanity, Freedom, and Endless Seeking. And as I give it back into his hand who entrusted me with it for a brief space, above all hard thoughts which you may have, above all misunderstandings, I hear one voice, which is enough: "It shall not return unto me void, but it shall accomplish that which I please, and prosper in the thing whereto I sent it."

NOTE.—The above sermon concluded my ministry in Washington City.

THE ONE PATH.*

First pure, then peaceable.

It is now eight weeks, and the Congress of these States, called, as if in bitter irony, *United*, is still unorganized. There is reason enough for the grave apprehension now pressing upon the mind of every patriot. Our young Hercules, just as his labors have arisen before him, and the nations looked on to see him strangle the Hydra here, and there unbar the flood of Reform toward manifold Augean stables, suddenly becomes paralyzed. O, son of Jove! last and strongest, what is this? whither has thy noble promise fled?

We meet here, my friends, on a common ground. Varied perceptions of the relations of that common ground to human welfare separate us into different parties. We are also of diverse sections. I do not think the pulpit should be used to assail any of these, as such. I, therefore, shall not permit myself a doubt, as I touch this most sensitive subject, that you will sympathize with me, and with each other. I do so

*Delivered in the City of Washington, January 26, 1856, during the contest for Speaker, which resulted in the election of Mr. Banks.

only because, in these troubled times, my heart burns to point you to the ancient landmarks of Right and Wrong, which, when seen, none can fail to acknowledge; for, like the objects of the ear and eye, they are their own evidence. I shall not make any partisan statement, for I belong to no party; but there is one phase of the present state of things which enters my pulpit, whether I will or not. This arc of the circle—not the arcs of the politician or economist—the pulpit cannot be true to itself without interpreting. And I am constrained to believe it a mathematical certainty, that any arc of any circle, moral or geometric, being given, the others may be discovered and described, and the radii traced to their center.

I shall waste no words on the dogma, that such subjects are not proper to the pulpit. Christ and Paul found them appropriate to *their* ministry. If moral questions should not enter here, what should? And if questions involving the happiness of millions, and the good relations of section with section, and man with man, throughout the land, are not moral, what are?

It was the saddest day that ever dawned on the country, when this was made any other than a moral question. In the day when it was made one of national political issue, the wind was sown; to-day we reap the whirlwind. It is exclusively a moral question, as are all questions affecting humanity. It is not a question of North and South — those very terms should be banished as unhealthy here. How completely do we find moral perceptions obscured, when here, in the noon of the nineteenth century, on a question involving more entirely than any other the just relations of men toward each other and toward God—a great nation is *geographically* divided. Men with divine souls must be lumped with the clod whereon they tread, and certain principles and ideas considered as exclusively products of certain sections, as coffee or cotton. Given a man's longitude and latitude, and you may predict his views on Slavery, and nearly everything else; as when you know the way the wind blows, you may announce with certainty the position of the nearest weathervanes.

But in the present state of things, the political view hears its trump of Doom. The old party watch-fires are but blackened earth and ashes; their lines have fallen in *un*pleasant places. A fearful disintegration has supervened the political mass: let us hope by the working of a higher synthesis. Hitherto we have had ancestral compacts and the political representation of negroes canvassed. Men have spoken of what is "wise and expedient," rather than what is right. You need not that any one should show you how this political treatment has miserably failed, even in objects no higher than its own. Each party has come forward with its nostrum, declaring itself the original old Dr. Jacob Townsend, whose pills, and none others, were genuine; each was to bring repose to the distracted patient, and soothe irritation by profounder nationality.

The inflammation has spread with every Administration until this; and with this, the very powers which enable inflammation to spread seem nearly death-still. I doubt not it would be so with the administration of any merely political party in the country. Let the people know, then, that this is the grand success of the *political* treatment of the Slavery question—every wheel of the government stilled!

In this state of things, it will not be the popular heart, but they who live by smothering that heart, who will withstand those who now, when all other methods fail, present THE ONE PATH, opened up before the country in the Christian Law, *First pure, then peaceable.* Every man knows how alone he gets peace. Priests may mumble over the souls of the departed, or beneath them, *Requiescat in pace*, but no soul ever rested in peace until it had entered it by the path of purity. And the greater is contained in the less; each atom obeys the laws of the sphere. Nations began with individuals, and are now but collections of them, and must obey the laws of individuals. With both, peace blossoms only on the stem of purity.

This, then, will save us from any national peril, that the Conscience shall be enthroned everywhere Absolute Monarch. It must be allowed untrammeled action, wherever, in any man, it prohibits slaveholding, and wherever, in any man, it does not, so far as any other than moral methods of restraint are concerned. Only let men feel that they are living and voting at unity with their best light of duty, and they demand no more, but are at ease. When agitation is abroad, it is certain that the lash of conscience has been loosened somewhere.

In order to secure this, we are called to mutual concession—to the concession of each moral sense to the other of all it claims—it being understood that nothing can be claimed by either for political advantage, but only from such a sense of the moral necessity of such a claim as shall never shrink from any results whatever, which are needed to secure it. If the two portions of the country cannot unite, and feel at the same moment ready to face the Eternal Judge, with the full conviction that they are each completely true to God, and to every man, white and black, bond and free, on earth, let them sink together beneath the waters under the earth, but never, never unite, or remain united!

We are called the more to this concession, because the error has been with both sides, and is now. The men whose consciences were first stirred on this subject have dwelt on the inhumanity of slaveholders, without remembering to ask whether THEY *were not slaveholders.* For whatever the Federal Government sanctions or adopts is of course by complicity of all who are parties to that Federal compact. As the people of Virginia did not derive their power to hold slaves from the Union, and do not now, of course none of the rest of the States, or of the individuals of the States, are involved in it. They are, indeed, in a high sense, *con-*

cerned in all that concerns their fellow-men; but not otherwise are they morally involved, than as they are in widow-burning in Hindostan, or cannibalism in the Fejee Islands. Do we, as Americans, take upon our consciences the sins, as we may think them, of Great Britain or Japan, because we have treaties with those nations? Do England and France become responsible for one another's policy, or assume each other's National Church, because, for a different object, they have formed an alliance? The United States are but such an alliance. And, as England and France have only a common responsibility for what is done in the war with Russia, so have the people of the free States only a responsibility for what is done by the Federal Union as such.

This blunder has had its antithetical one in the South. And here, I may say, we must guard against our prejudices. As a Virginian, with no tie of relationship northward, of the remotest kind, past or present, I feel how easily I might slide into a justification of my dear mother, the South. But the soul knows no prejudices or sections, and must see all under the pure light of reason and conscience.

The first error of the South has been an impatience in the discussion of this question, reminding calm men of those unfortunate persons met with in lunatic asylums, who speak rationally on all topics until you touch that on which they are deranged, when their insanity bursts wildly forth. This has caused them to put themselves in an attitude before the world which has brought down its severest censure; and, feeling that this was not just what they deserved—since they were at least sincere—it has led them on to a still greater rage against a judgment which, however unfair, was the result of their own mistaken heat. It has precluded freedom of discussion even among themselves; a policy which no human brain or heart ever respected yet. The native sons of the South have again and again sought to discuss it in their own vicinities, and have as often been threatened and visited with angry processes, though the privilege is secured them in the Bill of Rights of nearly every Southern State. The South has thus lost the confidence of many of her own children, who find that a freedom exercised by their lordly ancestors, Washington, Jefferson, Henry, and by them transmitted as an eternal inheritance, is now denied them by men who beside those are lilliputian. Those who deny that the full sunlight should play above, and beneath, and around any subject, can never convince any disinterested person that they are in the right. This was true before Jesus said, "Whoso doeth right cometh to the light," and it has been true ever since, and will be true to all eternity. What would men, including the South, say to Christ's getting into a passion with an antagonist, or Plato's refusing to hear the other side in an argument?

Blunder is of a prickly-pear growth, one leaf developed from another. This impossibility of free speech in the South has preserved a Code of Slavery which is far beneath her moral sense, but which cannot become a dead letter so long as there are wicked and selfish men in the world. As an evidence of this, it is a familiar fact that the wretched men termed "Negro-drivers," are held, with their families, in scorn by all classes of society in the South; yet no business is more entirely legal, necessary and remunerative.

How is the Code to be reformed, if it is a crime to broach the subject? Take any Southern man, and ask him if he believes that these blacks should be so completely in the possession of the whites that there should be no security to the marital relation; that one man should have the power, if he wills, to separate the families he owns to any extent? Ask him if he believes that immortal beings should be reared in brutal ignorance? (And those who do otherwise by their slaves break the laws. How sadly suggestive is the fact that the only other people who forbid education to any, are the Yezeddis of Mesopotamia, who are also the only race of devil-worshipers!) A Southern man will reply, NO.

And yet these laws remain there, trained by Southerners who are *not* men, to bear the cruelest fruits; such as have aroused the open indignation of the world, and the secret indignation of thousands of Southern hearts, and shall continue to do so, until human souls, North and South, are fatherless, and no divine instincts of justice and pity flow out from God's heart.

Thus both sides, by their own premises, need internal reform. But our reference now is to the great moral responsibility pressing on each, and growing out of our being one people. I would the pressure were heavier! In this country, where, by the very nature of the representative system, all action and influence of the General Government—involving as they do the happiness or misery, elevation or degradation, of men, women, and children, everywhere—are shared by every tax-payer and voter, the moral responsibility resting on each man is tremendous. What abject cant is it to say, The North has nothing to do with Slavery. Nothing to do with it! When the National flag cannot wave over a slave in this District, nor in any United States Territory, who is not a slave by Northern as well as Southern consent! Never was any duty plainer than theirs to attend to this affair—to see what it is which they, by their representatives, have been perpetually sanctioning and extending. There is need that the voice of the ancient prophet should be in every breath which stirs the free airs of Free States, crying to each man this day, "Arise; for this matter belongeth unto thee!"

I alluded just now to those who had assailed the Southern institution, and neglected the demonstrable fact that the first and (until attended to) the only assailable thing with them was their complicity in it. The only sin of these is a confused perception. But there is another class of real criminals. It is they who see

Slavery to be wrong, and see how they participate in it, and might free themselves from it, but suffer themselves to be overcome by its allurements. I have been ashamed to hear, in Boston, the descendants of the Puritans apologizing for Slavery. They thought a Southern man would like that. But no Southern man would like that! The Southerners, thank God, are not so bad; they say, Slavery is right; if not, there is no apology for it. John Randolph spoke their sentiment, when, pointing his finger at one such man in Congress, he said, "I envy not the heart nor the head of a man who can come here from the North and defend Slavery." Southern politicians are willing to make use of such, while they laugh in their sleeves; but the nobler men and women of the South grieve to see men falling thus meanly.

Here, at Washington, it has been as the fly in wheat—one noble head after another laid low; falling into infidelity, as the Slavery power has cast some web of interest around them. And those who believe, with Christianity, that it profits not a man to gain the whole world and lose his soul, turn pale and say, "Who falls next?" No matter if the concession is for "Peace." So did the army on the Alps desire nothing so much as peace, to lie down anywhere and sleep; and those who slept never woke more! Nothing is deadlier, at times, than peace; and invariably when, as in this case, the word Peace is but a cover of your desire, that your personal interest and business should be undisturbed—a disguise of that only Satan, Selfishness.

Ah, ye American men! too soon have you inscribed on your banner, *Peaceable.* More successful had it been, if the word had been in the order in which the ancient Christian places it—*first pure, then peaceable.* Never was there but one path given men to walk in—it is that of a pure conscience. Whether the light be dim or bright, it is in the right direction; guilt is in veering from that. There may be innumerable crooked lines between two points, but one straight. What is the right line between us and that peace we all crave?

We can all imagine two men of entire candor and courtesy — the one Southern, and believing Slavery right in itself; the other Northern, and believing it wrong—coming to an understanding on the subject; the common postulate being only that neither must himself do what he believes essentially wrong.

Southern.—I believe the institution is best for the white and colored races.

Northern.—I make no doubt of your sincerity, but would like to discuss it.

Sou.—We may do that presently. But will you not allow that, so long as I hold that opinion, you have no right of any kind to illegally interfere with what I hold legally as property?

Nor.—I do see that. The wrong is not in my detestation of Slavery, nor my endeavor to inspire you with a like feeling, but in my attempting a right thing in a wrong way.

Sou.—Which is always an unsuccessful way.

Nor.—Now, let us define the other side. I believe that Slavery is the "wild and wicked phantasy," that Brougham called it; or the "sum of all villainies," which Wesley pronounced it. You are connected with it sincerely, and, therefore, unless you have refused possible light, innocently; but if I am connected with it, I sin.

Sou.—Certainly.

Nor.—If you and I have partnership in a slave, your innocence does not exculpate me.

Sou.—Certainly not.

Nor.—If you seek to make me a party to anything which I hold wrong, you are guilty, even though you believe it right, unless you can first persuade me also that it is right.

Sou.—It is so.

Nor.—And if our firm cannot remain without involving me in this wrong, my one path is out of it. The firm must be dissolved.

Sou.—Assuredly.

Now, my friends, let us approach our national agitations thus simply and quietly. The people of the United States are a firm. Wherever the firm deals with Slavery, *all* deal with Slavery; and the General Government *has* dealt, and does now deal, with that local institution. I appeal to you, Southern men, is it not the only right thing for those who believe Slavery to be sinful, whether it be really so or not, firmly to declare themselves free from all share in it, if not by your concession, then by whatever means they can, *but certainly to do it?*

But, it is said, your fathers conceded this and that, and will you not stand by their compact?

If there be any compact, and it pledges me to what I feel wrong, shall I be judged by my father's light?

But if, in obedience to your conscience, you should injure this Union, you would cause great evils—evils greater than Slavery.

Evils are not sins. We do not wish to rid ourselves of our share in national slaveholding, as from an evil disease, but as a moral defection, as falsehood or theft would be. Evil is a part of God's law; for He says by every prophet, "I create evil." He is responsible for whatever evils ensue; we only for doing his will. Is not my soul his voice? And when I reject that voice, which assures me it is wrong to do this, is it not a sad lack of faith in Him? As one would say, "Thou, Infinite Being, didst bid me thus, but didst not foresee, as I do, that this and that evil would follow?"

Will you imperil the interests of thirty millions of whites for three or four of Africans?

The adages, reply the others, are very good: Honesty, even in the old Roman sense, embracing all that is just and true to God and man, is the best policy: Right never wronged any man. The interests of the three or four millions of negroes are not so near to us as the interests of the whites who hold them. Those we would but redeem from physical Slavery; but these we would redeem from what, by our creed, is far worse, the crime of enslaving them. If I rob you, you know, I am far worse off of the two.

"Then, if you think thus, we must separate. We think you in error, that you cannot think our institution right; or that even to say it is inexpedient, or an evil, does not define your view; that you must count it immoral. Certainly, nothing, however valuable, should induce us to do wrong; and the South admires, as much as any people, the brave words of Phocion, Let justice be done, though the heavens fall!"

But, it is replied, it does not end here. You say we must secede. But this proceeds from the assumption, that the Union is inextricably involved in the policy which makes all hold slaves. We do not believe that; we think the Union is essentially involved in Freedom, and that all its pro-Slavery proclivities are usurpations. We believe, indeed, that it does not interfere with you in your slaveholding, nor the English in their aristocracy, nor the Arabs in their Mohammedanism; but, at the same time we believe our Constitution protects us from compulsory sanction of these, and protects us in our freedom. Thus we cannot enlist against it, but only to redeem it from the distractions resulting from a misinterpretation of our compact. If there is secession, it cannot be on our side.

On this assertion, now made by a large portion of this nation in terrible earnest, hangs all the excitement, and will hang more and more. Crimination and violence serve no purpose here. Both are equally sincere. Individuals may be insincere, but no large mass of men can hold together, with means and influence, for any length of time, on an affected or fanatical basis. Hypocrisy would forbid the enthusiasm manifested on both sides; and the outlay necessary for a cause cools all fanaticism.

How, then, shall these be reconciled with each other, preserving self-truthfulness?

We must set aside here those who cry "Peace," when there is none. I, for one, have lost forever my faith in those self-styled conservatives, who would rely upon "putting down agitation." That cry has been sounded for a score of years, and with what success any one may see by going no farther than the House of Representatives. Stop agitation! So Xerxes forbade the sea to advance; so the Phœnicians shot arrows into the clouds when a storm arose; so an English gentleman wrote an elaborate treatise, showing conclusively that the Atlantic could never be crossed by steam, which went out to America in the first steamer. Stop agitation! Judging by late events in Kansas, one would say it is to take much more agitation than the country has yet known, to put down agitation.

No; this scab of Acquiescence, which you would bring over the sore, is not a cure, even if you could get it; the fester would only deepen more treacherously. Agitation is not the disease, but the friendly symptom which admonishes of disease. Eruption and fever are the health of a disease; a wise physician will never wish them to cease, but by the eradication of the underlying cause.

How, then, is Peace, which all love, and which is for the interest of all, to come?

Let St. James answer: By the wisdom which cometh from above, which is first pure, then peaceable. Let every man in the Union only feel assured that he stands beneath the sheltering wing of his country, A PURE MAN. Let men cease to see the National Flag discolored by what they believe dishonorable and wrong, and then be told they have nothing to do with it, when each stands with his share in the eye of God and man! Then shall that unrest, which is the sign of the strong lash of Conscience, cease! Then shall the word SLAVERY, that dirge of our woes, never more disorganize Congress, for it will be beyond Congress. I pity the Northern man who finds repose while his hand is binding slaves; still more the Southern man who would desire to have him find peace in impurity.

I know how large a number of good men in the North this position will offend. But I am ready to reiterate that, when their personal responsibility for the bondage of a man anywhere is past, Slavery only addresses them as other evils. A man cannot, of course, cease his testimony against whatever is to him wrong, except by being so far forth implicated in it. It may, however, be emphatically announced to this class, that if all they had ever thought, said, or written, on this topic—abstractly good, as much of it is—were condensed into one word, it would be to the act which would have freed them, or any one of them, from complicity in the thing, as a child's play to the great Lisbon Earthquake. If any of them thinks that the preservation of the Union involves such complicity, let him not turn phrasemonger, but himself secede, and rot in prison, ere he pays taxes or accepts advantages in his State through which he is inevitably involved. No eloquence would persuade like this. A great action is by its divine nature irresistible; great words are good only when difficulties make them great actions. In some way or other, nations are at the mercy of strong men, and a thousand flee before one. Truly, says the Brahmin:

> Devoutly speak, and men
> Devoutly listen to thee;
> Devoutly act, and then
> The strength of God acts through thee.

How godlike is it to be brave and true! There never was a soul conceived in God's mind, or projected into the North or South, or East or West, who in itself honored dapperness or cowardice, and respected not an honest, unflinching stand on any side. I am a Southern man, and I fear not contradiction from any one born there when I say that they all respect a man from the North who will not bend from his principles; and that not one of them thinks a doughface worthy to be valued as more than a catspaw. A heroic action for virtue, which is such only because imperiling large interests, is a new star lit in the Heavens. Men see it, and feel the presence of the unseen higher Power; they know with joy that the earth is more than a moving anthill. This joy cannot be moved by any danger or loss. If the Union were sundered by such a stand, does it not pay in that it props the whole Earth? For were the Union divided on a principle of right, a voice like the angel-hymn of a Second Advent would go forth, proclaiming the law by which thrones tremble, and all oppressions and evils fall as leaves in October,—First pure, then peaceable.

Before all, then, let us dismiss Fear. Let us, with Montaigne, fear nothing so much as fear. Southern men! Northern men! be one in being brave for your light and your right! If it should be found ever necessary to separate—as I pray I may never believe more than I do now—still would mutual honor survive; and by no event can any obstruction befall the vast destiny for which these superb American hills and plains were planned. By their great strength, these national throes proclaim the grandeur of a Nation's new-birth. Hark! there is now as of old a voice on the angry waters, "It is I: be not afraid." Serene and unharmed above our small cares and storms is enthroned the Genius in whose mind once, as in an egg, lay the Western Hemisphere, and Columbus, and Washington, and to our tearful prayer replies, O, man, think you that I have created these in vain? Know that until God is dethroned, the Right must prevail: Until He dies, nothing good can die!

THE LOST BOWER.*

SAY not thou, What is the cause that the former days were better than these?

MRS. BROWNING has entitled one of her finest poems The Lost Bower. A child goes forth to play among the trees, and follows wherever her wayward fancies lead. Presently she finds herself in the midst of a most beautiful bower: sweetly the vines cling about the young trees, which, rising around as pillars, intertwine branches and leaves above her head. Delighted she sits beneath the wondrous arch, and fancies that it must have been planned by the fairies. There the morning glides only too swiftly away over the enchanted child, who sits in the magic bower, beguiled by beautiful reveries and dreams. . . . Scarcely can she sleep for thinking of her new-found treasure, out in the grove. In the morning, what speed to find it again, and recall the beautiful fancies! Alas! she searches in vain. Every tree, every bush, every flower seems to stand where it was, but the bower cannot be found. Day

* Thanksgiving-day, Nov. 26, 1857.

after day, with tearful eyes, she searches; nay month after month, year after year—in vain; the lost bower takes its place among the sweet visions of the past—the loved and lost.

My friends, our lives are searches for lost bowers. We walk about in the present, but do not really live in it; that is, our bodies, our gayety, all that is most superficial about us, may be seen on the street and in the parlor to-day; but the *real life*, meditation, memory, feeling, thought, all that is most sacred in us, clings to the names and places of the past. There stand, in its "dim religious light," the forms of our heroes; our worship is the echo of two thousand years; we find no Eden short of six thousand. Who has not felt the charm of what is old? Who does not find in himself the explanation of how the word, which simply means what should be held sacred, has come to mean anything old, which is the case with the word *venerable?* Who does not know the awe which falls from old church music, and from gothic arches, which our age gathers from the past to associate with its most sacred hours, as we press in our Bibles the flower given by one now in the grave? Not all the blossoms of this year are so sweet, so beautiful as that poor faded leaf. Our whole lives are a sad silent inquiry, Why were the former days better than these?

But what had become of that lost bower? Wherefore could not the child find it again? Each tree, bush, flower stood there still. Whither had the fairy-vision fled? . . . Surely, it was the fabric of her own fancies! Her innocence, her faith, her heart of joy, were the fairies which wove the vines into lattice-work, and made the grass a divan. But such a day and bower, with its visions, did not leave her the same child that entered; the bower was there next day, next year, but the eyes were changed. The primer was lost because its lessons were learnt.

Search no more in the grove, fair child! forth where-ever thy destiny leadeth; in the school, in the home, faith and innocence shall rear bowers as beautiful; each day shall yield its own visions and dreams. The universe is pledged thee that no good is superseded but by a greater good: not loss, but gain is the law. The lost bower was but the unfailing artist's study of a grander design!

By an excellent custom of our country, we are called together to-day to consider "these days," not past days; to see what there is in the day now shining upon us for which to be thankful. Never were there times in which our faith could be better tested. We stand under shadows thicker than those which have clouded any Thanksgiving-day that even the oldest person who hears me can recall. The scars of one terrible war have not yet healed over, when the spice-laden winds of India are wafted to us, sickened with the scent of blood. The ocean has yawned again and again to swallow up its thousands, and drape unnumbered families with mourning. Our own land has fallen into the hands of irresponsible power, which, in the guise of Liberty, each day robs freemen of their most sacred rights; which answers our outcries with outrage on outrage; which gives to the children of a noble ancestry, when they ask for the bread earned by the bloody sweat of their heroic fathers, the stone and the serpent. The pillars which supported the fabric of a nation's trade have tottered, and we stand amid the ruins to-day, feeling that this hush of terror is too surely to be followed by the piteous cries which shall come from those who see no angel standing between them and the cold winter; who, penniless, fold their strong arms beside silent looms and cold furnaces.

As a people, then, how natural would it be, on this annual day, instead of pondering what we have to call forth thankfulness, to gather together, and weep over a nation's lost bowers; to inquire, Why were the former days better than these? How swiftly rush our thoughts back to the years of plenty; the long periods when no sound of war burdened the air; when our dear land was not torn by strife; when, alike in Massachusetts and Virginia, white was supposed white, and black, black,—right was right, and wrong, wrong; and the hopes of a world's emancipation beat high!

Yet a little reflection shows us that these advantages of those days, toward which we turn so longingly, were the merest illusions; else why did they not last? What is good is permanent; only what is false, or merely sentimental, perishes, or *can* perish. Take, for instance, the history of American freedom. It is common for us to recur to the period immediately succeeding the Declaration of Independence, as that in which the principles of Liberty were most acknowledged among us. Anti-Slavery men are pointed to large votes in favor of emancipation in several of the Slave States, as efforts which they have paralyzed: the declarations for freedom of the leading men North and South, at that time, are quoted. It is true, indeed, that this was the sentiment of the country; but it was *only* sentiment. The pecuniary interests of the country were not, to any material extent, involved in the institution of Slavery at that time; nor did our wisest ancestors see that they were to be, else never would they have quietly made the concessions to it which were made. As soon as the impulse for freedom was found in collision with these pecuniary interests, or supposed interests, it was proved a *mere impulse:* there was no man at the South, and for years none at the North, who was found to have it *as a principle.* It remained for *these days* to produce men willing to risk immediate interests, for what, in *former days*, was only a sentiment.

It is even so with the rest of our lost bowers. There were days when peace smiled on the land, and the temple of Janus was closed, to the world's joy; but how shallow a peace! a gay bubble, which the smallest pin-point could cause to vanish any instant! It takes tenfold the pressure to break peace, once gained, now—

tenfold of what was required in even the latest periods of the world. Every war deepens the sentiment into a principle, graven with fire on the popular heart. Sebastopol heralds, in thunder, the advance of the Prince of Peace!

Or is it the loss of credit and financial abundance that we deplore? It is demonstrable, that the financial crash is the special glory of this year. The ruin is a grand reality; the smooth prosperity of the "former days" of trade is now seen to have been a whited sepulcher, covering rottenness, and dead men's bones. Last year it was a glossy system of gambling and falsehood; to-day, thank God, we stand on truth; for truth is beautiful even amid ruins. I say again, it is the crowning glory of these days, that health enough remained to tear up by the roots this deadly upas tree, under whose poisonous shade so many of our young men had come and were coming to find repose!

Hear then the answer which the spirit of the present has for those who look backward and ask, Why were the former days better than these? You are "these days;" if they are not better, it is because *you* are not better! All that the former days had, you have around you now; not one leaf of the lost bower has stirred: the beauty of Peace has not been dimmed; the eternal principle of Freedom has lost no luster; the laws of supply and demand, the necessities of trade are unchanged; gold is still gold, and iron, iron; the earth has not ceased to bear, nor seasons to roll on; the materials of all "former times" are furnished without stint to the hand of "these."

> "The fault, dear Brutus, is not in our stars,
> But in ourselves, that we are underlings."

Nay, see what we have in addition to all that the greatest foregone generations had: we have the deeper values which experience writes on everything: what to them were sentiments, have, with us, through fearful storms and bleak winds of human experience ripened to inviolable laws; dreams have been shaped into facts; each ingot of gold, each bar of iron has, under the command of the stern Cromwell of Knowledge, descended from its niche, ready, as we shall bid them, to be apostolic, and "go about doing good." The bowers which fairy sentiments planned for our ancestors, to pass away with the morning mist, the sturdy sinews of to-day may, if they will, realize in enduring granite. Indeed the mishaps and grievances which we bear to-day, are the upshot of what these much-lauded "former days" have bequeathed us; but it is in the power of the Genius of the Present to sow the dragon's teeth of Evil, and gather the harvest of a phalanx for God; to enthrone Peace on the ruins of War; to see the Samson of Slavery buried by the action of his own blind power; to convert the angry flood of a financial crisis into a fit moment for turning the stream into more natural and lawful channels, wherein the golden argosies of commerce shall be borne on before healthier breezes than those that fill the sails of Wall Street.

II. But I am jealous of every moment which detains us from interpreting this law as it prevails in the private heart. Each one who has the key to the facts of his own experience, has the key to all public facts—a single heart being the moral world in miniature, as a drop of dew is the sphere in miniature, with its own equator and magnetic poles.

How unconsciously do our eyes, when the immediate care which had claimed them has passed, look longingly to our past. The quiet hour of solitude has fled: it may be summed up as a reverie in which the old forms and faces reappeared; memory delivered us to memory, and we are recalled to life only by the starting tear. The life around us seems strange and foreign; there in the old school-room, the old yard, under the mother's caress, the real life lingers. The home-woe clings to us. We pass through the present as a wilderness, and often, with the children of Israel, we hang our harps upon the willow and weep when we remember the holy places we have left, for how shall we sing the heart's songs in a strange land? I have often felt the room grow very still as some one sang "Auld Lang Syne," or "By-gone Hours," or "I Would I Were a Boy Again." The popular Ballad-poetry of all nations turns generally toward the past.

The instinct is delicate and true. The old bowers would not have been made so enchanting, had it not been meant we should seek for them. For there lies the sunlit shore of *happiness:* our childhood knew no sorrow, as we know sorrow now, in the days when "every grief and every pain were wept away in transient tears." One tender kiss could cure all. The heart which now cannot be quite happy without some contribution from every continent and every island on the planet, was happy then with a doll or a top, and found the wealth of Ormus and of Ind in a baby-house or a coasting-hill. . . . Better yet; back there is the moon-lit realm of *dreams*,—dreams whose gorgeous sheen had not turned to cold night-fog in the garish daylight of knowledge. What superb lives we lived with Jacob and Joseph, Mary and the young child, Solomon and Sheba's Queen for our personal friends; how proudly we walked the golden cities and fair islands of the realm of the good and great Haroun Al Raschid; what voyages we took, what magnificent sights we saw with Sinbad! Alas for the day when we awoke and rubbed our eyes again, but saw that there was no ladder let down from heaven, saw that Haroun Al Raschid reigned no more, saw that our poor society was made up of far other elements than Valentine, and Fortunatus, and the seven Champions! . . . Sweeter yet; back there is the serene blue heaven of *Faith* bending over our childhood. No cloud of doubt had overcast, nor rained down its chill upon our hearts. God could be seen and loved in the father and mother. Why should we look tremblingly into the future, when the Ever Near was there to supply our wants through their hands? No Medusaworld stood there staring us in the face, freezing the genial currents of instinct and truth by threats of loss and persecution. Thou beautiful trust of childhood, where art thou now in this, our cautious, calculating life! . . . Above all, O, above all! there are the blessed isles of *Innocence.* For once, thank Heaven, we stood in the world clothed with the snow-pure raiment of stainlessness! Press down on our heads heavily as ye will, dark memories of sin, ye cannot rob us of the sacred tears, through which, as lenses, we see at our life's morning a child, arrayed in white, glistering, transfigured!

Ah! who shall rebuke us if seeing all these in our past we ask sadly, Why were the former days better than these?—if, even on our day of Thanks, we turn away from all we have and are to search for our lost bowers?

Happiness, the ideal life, entire trust, innocence;—rich indeed the coronet of gems on childhood's brow! Yet, let us inquire into these as they existed in us in those "former days." What is that *happiness* which is not conscious of its own existence? Is it not as a white figure against a white back-ground? And where is this dark back-ground which the white form of happiness needs, in order to be known as such, to be found? The happiness of a child is the mere negation of sorrow; it is not positive; it does not feel the thrill which pleasure must derive from contrast with pain. We continually see that the child is ignorant that the older persons around yearn toward its happy Kingdom: it yearns just as much toward maturity, and often shows impatience of the slow years. . . . Beautiful also are these air-castles and dreams of the young; so also are the blossoms beautiful,—yet well may the eye which weeps over their fall, smile as it looks up and sees the fruit ripening in their place. An air-castle turns to old gray stone, unless it can be lived in; and the Arabian Nights create a craving for Arabian days, a craving which they cannot satisfy. . . . Also that *faith* of the child: what is that trust which has never been tested? We also, in our maturity, could have such faith as that, if to our every desire a hand came forth for its satisfaction. Easy is it to have faith, when faith and sight are one; easy to trust when the sun shines bright and all is gay: but to trust when all is dark, to believe when there is no sight, to live by faith when it draws near to the shadow of death,—*that* is something higher, nobler than all the sunny, cloudless sky shining over childhood. . . . .

Thus much also must we say of the child's innocence. It too is merely a negation, not a positive good: it does no harm, but the question presses, What good does it do? Sugar is sweet, but one cannot live on sugar. We sicken on it, and long to have some kind of flavor dropped upon the lump. The fall from innocence is the knowledge of good and evil; to deplore that our first parents ever ate of that tree of knowledge, is to deplore that they ever rose above being mere animals. The first deep trace of character was drawn then.

Not then, as they existed in the "former days," are happiness, the dream-life, faith and innocence to be desired. Shall we, then, never find the lost bower? . . . Friend, to copy the fair visions of former days into the actual life of these days, seems to be the true aim. Nothing is lost; nay, how much is gained! Did childhood ever feel the joy—I will not call it happiness — the thrilling joy with which, in some great moment, you have looked up through earth's shadows, and felt that God lived;—heard his mighty heart beat *for you?* . . . Look you, can the highest, fairest dream of your childhood match the blue sky, as seen in some serene moment, which followed trial? or Sinbad's diamond valley, does it compare with the star-sown garden of God above you, as caught by the eye, which experience of earth's pettiness has lifted upward? . . . Tell me, could all your trustfulness toward your parents, gathered from all your earlier life, be thought of, when, in freedom and faith, you have scorned a worldly prudence, and spoken the word, done the deed for God, then felt that, in the same moment, his arm was folded around you as a mother's, and all the tears that men could wring from you, were received in his bosom? . . . And for innocence, what so white and true as that which can do no harm, because it is absorbed in doing good? For the soul, which is filled with a noble enthusiasm for noble work, is lifted from the plain of shadows, and whatever its stains, in its divine passion, is spread under the all-bleaching sun, which withers up the faintest spot or blemish.

There was one who went forth to seek his lost bower. As he searched, one met him—a tender face, which seemed to float in the dreamy memories of "former days." "Sir, if thou hast taken it hence, tell me where thou hast borne it." "Was it not reared of happiness, of ideals, of faith and innocence?" "It is the same." "Then, my child, I can lead thee there." So they went on, hand pressed in hand, till they stood, O joy! before the lost bower! But now, from the lindens, from each flower's calyx, came forth ministering spirits. The rose said: "Thou seekst again the bloom of joy. Ask and receive, that your joy may be full." The lindens sang, "Thou seekst the old land of dreams. Eye hath not seen, nor ear heard, neither have entered the heart of man the things which God hath prepared for those that love Him. But his spirit revealeth all." The sparrows in their boughs chirruped sweetly: "Seekst thou thy childhood's trust? Behold, not one of us 'is forgotten before God;' and 'thou art of more value than many sparrows.'" Then said the pure white lilies: "Seekst thou the child's innocence? 'Thus saith the Lord, Though your sins be as scarlet, they shall be as white as snow; though they be red like crimson, they shall be as wool.'" And over the doorway was written: "Except ye shall become little children, ye cannot enter." Then that seeking spirit knelt before him who had led it there, and knew that hallowed head; that loving face. "To whom shall I go but unto thee, O Lord? Thou hast the words of eternal life." Then there, in the bower regained, in the Eden which is not the dream of "former days," but the reality of the present, that soul found its Thanksgiving-day.

Is the bower lost then? Who sayeth
That the bower indeed is lost?
Hark! my spirit in it prayeth,
Through the solstice and the frost;
And the prayer preserves it greenly, to the last and uttermost,
Till another open for me,
In God's Eden-land unknown,
With an angel at the doorway,
White with gazing at His throne;
And a saint's voice, in the palm trees, singing,
"All is LOST . . . and WON!"

THE COMMUNICANT.

He then, lying on Jesus' breast, saith unto him, "Lord, who is it?" Jesus answered, "It is he to whom I shall give this morsel when I have dipped it." And when he had dipped the morsel, he gave it to Judas Iscariot.

Can it be possible? Can this be the true reading of the record, that Jesus gave the awful Eucharist of the Church to a man in whose face he read treachery, avarice, and malice? Did he not recoil, and did not his face contract to a frown, when, on that memorable evening of the Last Supper—the last time in which he should meet with them all—it came Judas' turn. The account says not—and that too after passing through the severest crucible of doubt and test, in every century, since it was written. Christ stands committed to having given Judas the communion bread and wine without hesitation or qualification.

Looking on that household work of art, Leonardo da Vinci's painting of the Last Supper, we find ourselves attracted by two faces; one is the trustful, tender St. John—we are at once touched to gentleness and love; the other is the scowling Judas—we are inflamed with indignation and scorn. As we turn then to the face of Jesus, we are struck with the happy genius which has preserved the real superiority of him to all others; for the face of Christ, looking on Judas, has not lost the tenderness with which it looked just now on John; it does not partake of our indignation. He reflects not the scowl of that man who grasps the money-bag; and when he gives him the bread and wine, perhaps never so fully do we feel him to be the child of our Father in Heaven; for He maketh his sun to rise on the evil and on the good, and sendeth rain on the just and on the unjust.

I am aware how astonishing it is in the light of ecclesiastical history. Either Jesus was wrong in giving this sacrament to Judas, or every Church has been wrong in its administration. Scarcely had Christ and his immediate disciples died, when a vail of mysticism was cast about the Lord's Supper, which even the highest Protestantism has failed to withdraw fully. It has partaken the gradual stages of human culture and religious freedom. In one age, we find it the peculiar privilege of the priesthood. It is then, after controversy, decided, that the laity may receive it in one kind only, the priest taking both kinds. But great professions and sanctity must precede the admission of the devotee. As reformations, which can never cease their onward march, amid social and religious systems, until solar systems cease to move, have advanced, we have seen the masses admitted to this sacrament; but under such terrible injunctions and fearful denunciations of those who partake it in unworthiness, as to keep away all but those who regarded themselves as peculiarly sanctified. It has been always held as a terrible means of spiritual despotism, and excommunication regarded as an earthly anticipation of the final sentence, Depart ye cursed. Nearly all ministers reserve to themselves the right of refusing the communion to any one whom they consider unworthy; and it would, perhaps, be hard to find an ecclesiastic who does not show by his conduct that had he been in Christ's seat at the Last Supper, he would have passed by Judas with the bread and wine, and given it to all the rest. But Christ was not a churchman, and were he to appear now in any church, would be denounced as a schismatic.

And, my friends, though in our simple form of Church regulation no such priestly domination and passing upon others are possible; I do not think we have generally returned to the primitive spirit of the Sacrament. When I see at its stated return the division of the congregation which occurs; the pew-door opened, and the children and younger members of the family retiring; many leaving who, I know, secretly love and revere Christ and his religion, though counting themselves unworthy to say, "I am a Christian." O, when I see this, I feel that the meaning, the life-blood of the sacrament is lost, until it has become a mummied mockery; that what was to be a bond of union between all men, has become a line of division; that it means something in the minds of those who leave which we who participate will not acknowledge, and cannot without spiritual arrogance!

Let us this day come to an understanding of this service, and of each other. Let our motto, as a society, be the words of Orestes,—Between us be truth! And I would declare here and now, that I cannot regard the sacrament in any light which would prevent its being taken by every man, woman, and child in this house; and am unwilling to participate except under this avowal. Let us to-day withdraw the mystical hood which it received from hooded friars; and looking earnestly, see what was meant by it: and thus, unbinding hand and foot of their grave-clothing, may we find this institution throbbing with that life, without which it will soon be putrid.

I. I wish to examine the sources of error on this subject.

The phrases, This is my body—This is my blood, have often been used to inspire awe, even where the Romish idea of transubstantiation does not prevail. It has been thought, almost universally, to indicate some preternatural import in the service. But Christ is more of a poet than a technologist, and this is a phrase addressed to the imagination. The saying, "This is my body, and this my blood," is entirely in keeping with other phrases whose meaning is apparent: "I am the vine;" "the shepherd;" "the door of the sheep."

They are all, simply, oriental metaphors. The perversion of them dates to an age which invested the material person of Jesus with peculiar sanctity, akin to that which afterward, and even yet, exalts him metaphysically, separating him from the human brotherhood. A spiritual age can regard the idea of the real flesh and blood, only as religious cannibalism; and all other ideas as tinctured with it, except the spiritual and rational.

But the real sword of flame which has guarded the entrance to this table, has been a strong passage written by Paul to the Church at Corinth,—than which I do not know any human utterance more misinterpreted; and that, after being fearfully mistranslated. The facts are about thus:

Corinth, more than any city of that period, was noted for its wealth, luxury, and dissoluteness. The corruptions of the city had crept into the Christian Church at that place. This first began to be manifest in the observance of the Lord's Supper. The members of the Church were in the habit of bringing with them at the time of its recurrence, bread and wine for its celebration. When Paul had left them, they brought more than was necessary for the emblematic character of the rite. We learn from St. Paul's epistle, and it is easy to believe concerning such a city and age, that, by gradual corruption, this simple and solemn feast became a banquet. The poor were excluded from a table to which they had not the means to contribute; and those who did attend, feasted to excess, and even drunkenness; thus surrounding the Christian communion with the scenes of the pagan saturnalia, which they had professed to relinquish. In reference to these abuses, Paul writes: "Now in this that I declare unto you, I praise you not that you come together; for it is not for the better, but the worse. When ye come together, therefore, it is not to eat *the Lord's* Supper: for in eating every one taketh before other his *own* supper; and while one is hungry, another is drunken. What! have ye not *houses* to eat and to drink in? or despise ye the Church of God, and shame those who have not?"—that is, have not the means to contribute to the rich feasts. After reminding them of the simple meaning of the ordinance, he adds: "He that eateth and drinketh unworthily, eateth and drinketh damnation to himself, not discerning the Lord's body;" that is making it a means of sensuality, rather than spirituality.

How many millions have refused to unite in this service because of this word "damnation," no man can compute. The word is one which is not translated "damnation" elsewhere in the Testament, and occurs several times in this very connection without being so mistranslated. It really means that those who ate and drank in this excess, ate and drank that which harmed them rather than benefited. You will readily see, too, that the entire spirit and phraseology are addressed to a state of the world and the Church, which could not exist at the present time in any part of Christendom, and therefore cannot be properly used as they have been.

Yet there is a form in which we may well be addressed by the words, Whoso eateth and drinketh unworthily, eateth and drinketh harm unto himself. Most eagerly do we announce, that if any one partake the communion from an unworthy motive,—not meaning thereby anything but a cover, or a desire of approbation, or a self-commendation to the community, he is doing that which shall let loose the lash of conscience upon him!

But the phrase is "unworthily," not "in unworthiness." If it be interpreted to excommunicate all who feel deeply their unworthiness to be called Christians, those who, conscious only of need, are unwilling to make any open professions of Christianity—then let us all retire. The saints may take it exclusively for themselves. I, for one, cannot touch it. Who can?

But when I remember one who said, "Do this and remember me;" that he dipped the morsel, and gave it alike to John, who loved, and Peter, who denied, and Judas, who betrayed—I can draw near, as one who sometimes may love, and yet oftener denies and betrays. And the heart replies: "O, weak and straying child! this is given thee *because of thy unworthiness.* Thy sin and thy need alone keep it from being a dead form."

II. Now then, that there are no more any traditional errors in our minds on this subject, we may find greater freedom in the positive side of our subject—this, namely, What is the exact significance of this sacrament to men; not to saints, nor communicants, nor baptized persons alone, but to the common heart—to men?

It lies in one thing—and one which is as comprehensible to one man as to another—one which appeals to old men and women, and young men and women; to boys and girls, and newly-weaned babes; to thieves and gamesters, and swearers and idlers. That one thing is SELF-SACRIFICE. It is the alpha and omega of Christ's life and teachings. The contribution of his life to the human soul, was a broken body and shed blood—the only interest about which is the self-sacrifice they imply. The injunction of his religion and its offer is a yoke, a burden, a cross—the only thing which elevates these above the yoke of the ox, the burden of the slave, the cross of the criminal, is the self-sacrifice they symbolize. One thing is forever sublime and god-like; that is heroism, and heroism is self-sacrifice. Beautiful is self-sacrifice at home, where each gives up something for other's happiness; in the manifold forms of love, and of unselfishness: sublime is it in nations, where mutual concession preserves justice and peace: god-like is it in the hero, who for a principle will sacrifice wealth and position, or will drink the sacrament in dying for the right—drinking of the same cup, and baptized in the same baptism, with him who instituted it.

A sad day was it for the Church, when a fierce and

thoughtless Puritanism dragged from every steeple the only real symbol of Christianity—the cross. Would to heaven it now glittered from every steeple of church, or chapel, or temple, or mosque, or turret, or pagoda on the earth—silently writing on the sky, bending over every land and sea, the noblest word Paul ever uttered, "God forbid that I should glory save in the cross!" There let it be raised—there let it stand forever. Not to symbolize the ignorance of the past; not to preach absurd ideas of vicarious or imputative atonement; but to rouse in every man that deepest soul in every man, which knows that holiest of all in man or angel is *sacrifice;* that it is better to give than receive—to minister than be ministered unto; and that when, through forthcoming ages, "the thoughts of men 'have' widened with the process of the suns," and the earth has been subjected, in every element, to the dominion of man, and redeemed from her dungeon of evil, then nothing shall be found in the worlds grander than a soul, which loves God and man above self!

And from this time to that, there cannot be any moment in which self-denial is not demanded of every soul. To sustain to-day, and here the simple truth and purity of the Christian idea, apart from the dogmas and errors of men, demands it. To sustain the principles of justice, humanity, and freedom, so constantly trampled under foot in our presence, demands it. . . This bread and wine have the simplest voice, the voice of the Good Shepherd, saying to all, even the little children, and with as much tenderness and meaning for one as another: "If any man will come after me, let him deny himself, and take up his cross, and follow me!"

By this essential element, every duty is united; and the loftiest efforts and designs of the most enlarged philanthropy, are not wrought out by any law different from that whereby a child does an unselfish act to its brother, though only a toy be concerned, in one case, and a nation in the other. And in this spirit, which it symbolizes, we have the highest kind of *real presence*. The man who should resolve that he will live for others more than himself; that he will give what help he can to the poor; that he will seek to be unselfish as toward his family and neighbor—may not be willing, indeed, to say, I am a Christian; but he has received the highest benefit of the sacrament—a benefit far greater than if he thought he had eaten the actual body and blood of Christ, or that there had been some mysterious favor done heaven, which it would repay, which is the usual idea.

Then a little child can have the fullest appreciation of the sacrament, when it knows that it means that habit of self-denial which is the great lesson of childhood. How many, if their young minds were taught this simple lesson, and they were encouraged to take the bread and wine, would be impressed more thereby than by all other teaching? A religious light would shine on all their little associations; they would be kinder to one another, more forbearing, obedient, unselfish—doing this in remembrance of him.

III. Now, who will say that this principle, the mother of all other principles, which enters where love enters—human or divine love—is confined to any one class of the community? We know that there is no one who does not know that self-denial is the path of the Christian. I do not believe there is any one who is not conscious that it has its constant violations in his life. But there is likewise a certain internal knowledge, that nothing is so good as love and truth. And this germ within us, the Great Teacher would feed with those living streams, which flow from the example by which he has ennobled the cross. By remembering how to attest the truth, he did not shrink from any agony, we may well be led to put to ourselves some severe questions: How much of what I know is right, am I willing to stand by to my loss? How much farther would I follow the truth I hold, if I saw it lead to death by cross or otherwise? Is my life good and sweet; and should I this day fall into the grave, would it be written above, He lived a life of self-sacrifice? or of self-seeking? Are there none given to me, that in devotion to them, I may find myself?

When you have found that the sunlight falls only in the churches, and the regular communicants' houses, then may you deny the universality in some stage of their growth of those sentiments to which this sacrament appeals. I would not like to take upon myself the blasphemy of saying, that in God's universe, it is possible that a spirit can exist in which there may not be found something to which this central light of Christ is related. That a purely evil intelligence can exist in earth, or heaven, or hell, is to dethrone goodness, and circumscribe its destiny. "Every knee shall bow at last," is the higher creed of Paul; and faith repeats on earth the high hope of olden prophecy: "And in the last days, it shall come to pass, that the temple of the Lord shall be established on the top of the mountain, and all realms shall flow unto it."

And for this reason, because none can be beyond the reach of limitless love — because no heart can be so poor a hovel that no heavenly beam shall shine through its window—this memorial of the highest human devotion and love must be offered to all. When it is participated by a few, or any class or age is uninvited, then is it taken out of the entire spirit of Christianity. For we are too apt to forget that Jesus lived mainly with the very class of persons to whom this sacrament has been so long refused. Much scandal was created by his breaking bread with publicans and sinners. He never lost sight of the immortal soul in any one. And when the poor weeping Magdalen was brought before him, and the Jews were ready, by their law, to stone her to death, a glance drove them away; then, with a tenderness that restored the angel in her, he said; "I do not condemn thee; go, sin no more." It was the high mission of the Son of God to rise with blessed light full on all, and like some sweet moon, to draw by mysterious and beautiful light and love the tides of all souls, causing energies and aspirations, long stagnant or pent, to beat full toward the celestial shores.

O man! O, many-sided human heart! how little knoweth each of the other! Every soul knoweth its own burden, its bitterness, prayer, love, and hope; but dreams not it could be fully sympathized with by any other. If the vail could only be removed, and it could be seen that everywhere soul answers to soul, as, in a mirror, face answers face; if it were revealed to us how within us all are the same dreams and phantoms, hopes and doubts, heights and depths, strengths and weaknesses—I think we should fall on each other's necks with tears, as those who, walking a crowded thoroughfare, sunddenly meet face to face a brother or son whom they imagined in another continent. We should unite at this table, feeling that our need and weakness make us brothers; and if any Judas come here, to him also must we kindly, eagerly give the morsel. . . . For who is worthier to receive it? Not I. Who has not betrayed, from timidity or interest, Christ, or his conscience, the perpetual Christ, in instances which memory calls to witness against us? And yet there is nothing practically good which results not from our imperfections and poverty. Prayer is a sign of it; praise is enkindled by it. All that in us sees something higher to which we have not attained, is at once our glory and our shame. And this glorious yearning for somewhat high, nobler—be it weak or strong, be it in a good or evil man—is the divine title to this sacrament. You need not tell me you have no such inward craving. As well say you are living without lungs or blood. There it is, deep within you—flashing faintly forth perhaps, yet inherent; despair is a form of it, as well as hope. It goes on chanting forever in all:

Nearer, my God, to Thee—
Nearer to Thee!
E'en though it be a cross
That raiseth me;
Still all my song would be,
Nearer, my God, to Thee—
Nearer to Thee!

Though like the wanderer,
The sun gone down,
Darkness be over me,
My rest a stone;
Yet, in my dreams, I'd be
Nearer, my God, to Thee—
Nearer to Thee!

There let the way appear,
Steps unto Heaven;
All that thou sendst to me
In mercy given;
Angels to beckon me
Nearer, my God, to Thee—
Nearer to Thee!

See there that man with the evil shadow on his face! The disciples gaze at him with horror; cry, "Satan has entered him;" shrink from contact with him. But thou, blessed Saviour, didst not shrink nor turn from him! Thine eye pierced beneath the cloak of evil and treachery, and saw within the indestructible flame of God—dim indeed, and growing dimmer, but still an immortal spirit. Not to the hand or lip of Judas, but to that almost expiring soul, thou didst give the morsel. And thy love was not lost even on Judas.

As he went out into the dark night to perform the dark crime, there arose on his night one whitened spot—the vision of a tender face, which, seeing his evil design, still loved him; which, when it beheld the treachery in his heart, was not blackened with an angry cloud, but for a thunderbolt gave him the last token of affection in the emblems of that body so soon to be nailed to the cross by the very hand which received them!

O, I doubt not, this vision lingered with him and followed him when he "went out and it was night." I doubt not some far-off voice within him cried, when he was with Christ's enemies, "Did *he* love thee best, or did *these?*" By night and by day, waking, sleeping, there was before him the last he had seen of him, whom he had started so earnestly to follow; there it was—the face serene and full of love, while others frowned,—the hand holding out to him the morsel.

It was that act, that love which saved him! Had Christ arisen when the traitor entered and indignantly cried, "Depart, false heart! Pollute us not with thy presence!"—then he would have left with hellish mockery, and no pursuing angel. But now Love, beyond all that poor Judas had ever known, is hard after him. And ah, see! it has conquered him! When none were found to bear witness to the innocence of Christ, Judas proclaims it; and that penitence, so deep that death alone could relieve it, outweighs, let us trust, the dark sin!

So you will see, friends, how it is that I cannot dismiss you until the communion is over. I wished to explain this more fully. My benediction would choke me; I could not dismiss one single one of you, however unworthy, more than he, whom I would love to follow, could send away from the Last Supper, the man who betrayed him.

Rather would I say to you whose hearts cry with Judas, I have sinned in that I have betrayed the innocent—that cry finds its pitying ear here: And ye who cry with the Centurion, "Lord, I am not worthy that thou shouldst come under my roof,"—lo! he is already under thy roof! O my treacherous heart! O feeble will! To whom should I go but unto thee, O Lord! Thou hast the words of Eternal Life!

May the vision never leave us unpurified,—the vision of a love manifested through the tender, manly Christ, which ever flows from the heart of God to each and all, like the rain which he maketh to fall on the just and the unjust. No man can get beyond unlimited love. We may make larger or narrower the bed in our hearts for the fountain's play, but we did not cause it to flow, and we cannot cause it to cease. To these immortal cisterns, O brother-pilgrims, weary and athirst, let us repair,—with these waters are purity, and love, and everlasting joy.

THE CATHOLIC IDEA.

EVERY several gate was of one Pearl.

WHEREVER earnest religious Faith enters, the tendency immediately is to affinity and unity. The high nature of religion is at once *felt* to be superior to technical differences and petty disagreements. The appearance of Christianity was the signal for an effort to *unite* the Jews, long sundered into sects and scattered throughout the earth. And it was when the earliest persecutions of the Christian Church were suspended for a space, and each band was glowing with its first love, that it was found so easy to unite them all under one central head into a Holy Catholic Church. It were very wide from the truth to suppose that this union was for any but the highest purposes. They were all what they claimed to be by the word *Catholic*, *i. e. liberal*, *broad*, *universal*. Then was the Church a living thing, and its catholicity real.

Ah, had she only gone on in the same spirit with which the union had been baptized! But the Church did not see beyond its own immediate welfare; she did not see that those who came afterward in the ever-widening world, with the trust of larger views of all things which they were commissioned to make good to mankind, had an equal claim on her catholicity; such a catholicity, also, as should not deprive them of their birthright to individual freedom and thought. So the Church was soon proved not to be up to its own idea—the Catholic Idea—and so its history is heart-rending. But let us not hastily accuse it for this. What church *is* up to its idea? Does not each represent that idea, on which it claims to be based, only so far as is found convenient? Does Protestantism still bear a spirit of protest,—or does it settle down, as if no new ray should ever dawn upon the world? Even in our own church, which attracts so many of the thinking youth of this age, on account of its freedom, do we not see in some places signs of trammels and creeds?

And yet, though unrealized, there above us shines forever the great Catholic Idea, the vision of a united and powerful Christendom! There, on the pages of prophecy, gleam still the unfulfilled golden visions of the Church, prepared by purity and love as a bride for her Lord. The idea is always alive. Each young man, whose soul is dedicated to the highest purposes of life, feels the hope kindled within him; his instinct heralds unity; he is pained at anything like controversy in the pulpit; the criticisms of his parents and friends on other denominations grieve him as illiberal and unwarranted. Yet, as time goes on, he becomes in turn as querulous and particular as the rest; not through having surrendered his genial faith, but through having tried it and found it trampled underfoot of the herd. The angel Peace, once driven by the thirst for conquest from the kingdoms of the world, had sought the holy altars of the Prince of Peace; but soon Constantine's sword put her to flight, and though all hear in dreams the rustle of her wing hovering near us, yet she visits not the Church on earth.

It is not because the churches *really desire* to remain at strife thus. Indeed there is much evidence that the bitterest ecclesiastical quarrels have been caused by efforts at coming together. Every age witnesses an attempt at meeting, which only ends in a greater rebound.

About ten years ago, the churches of the world were called to unite in an Evangelical Alliance. It spanned the angry floods of controversy,—a bow of promise. At the Synod of Berlin, held by all denominations in Germany, preliminary to that of England, the leading spirits in which were the great-souled leaders of those called Orthodox, Neander and Tholuck, the latter gave the key-note of that religious union, for whose rich harmonies to burst upon the world, every ear of every land waited eagerly. In that Synod arose that most eloquent living preacher of the Reformed Church, and announced thus the central idea of the world's Evangelical Alliance: "The substantial unity of the Church, is a thing which already exists, and the Evangelical

Alliance has only to proclaim it to the world. All who are here must deplore the differences which exist in Christendom. But how can you put an end to them? You must make the attempt only in the way of mutual instruction and encouragement. In one of the Reformer's words, I will say there is no church, no Christian party which can claim to possess pure truth,—truth absolute in all points of view; and, if these words are true, I shall take the liberty of adding, that there is no church, no Christian party on the earth which may not learn something from the other churches and parties. It is thus we may realize a grand and true union, of which we see now only the commencement."

Well, in this high spirit the assembly gathered in London. Alas, the spirit was willing, but the flesh was weak; the lower dogmatizers triumphed over the superiors. The alliance could only be organized on a test creed of nine dogmas, which excluded the Catholic, Quaker, Swedenborgian, and Unitarian Churches. Thus an Evangelical Union could not be held in the noon of the nineteenth century, without the exclusion of two thirds of those who honestly believe themselves Christians! The result of the movement was a sad failure, and a speedy departure of the clergymen back to their parishes, to find the relighted flames of controversy burning fiercely on every altar in the world.

Now, these men did not go to England to produce such results. Each one who went there, doubtless thought that he comprised more brotherly kindness in his single self than any ten men who could be found in the alliance. Yet they forgot all when it was proposed to admit the Unitarian and Quaker delegates. What then is the difficulty? Why, it would seem that, though Christendom is conscious of a great want, it is not so clear as to the real nature of that want; and so it can only grope for the remedy. It cannot see yet that the Catholic Idea is the only one on which a true alliance can be based; and that, by its very nature, that would have to wipe out those last nine articles with which they must, they thought, burden men's minds; for this idea must take in all who love Christ's religion, no matter what articles they subscribe: the word catholic means UNIVERSAL.

And, though as yet we see no true embodiment of the Catholic Idea, we have, in the inspired words of the Seers, the study of this great design of the Highest. Behold there, on the lonely Island of Patmos, exiled by the decree of Domitian, one who, in his life, had leaned on the holiest breast, through which he had heard the beatings of that great loving heart of all things, whose care cannot be dissuaded from the smallest of his creation. He sits there, never less alone than when alone, in converse with ever-glorious unseen beings, for such are pure and divine thoughts. These build for him the towers of endless vision; for him, earth, sea, sky come close to whisper the superb raptures of that higher world of which his lonely Patmos was but the porch or outer-court. Ah, then, as some auroral arch leaps quivering athwart the northern midnight, so full on his eyeballs burst the burning, ineffable splendors of the City of God, the Church triumphant and united, the new Jerusalem purified and exalted!

One thing he saw, and repeats again and again—*Every several gate of that Holy City was one pearl!* This I must take as the type of our new and ideal Catholic Church; and I shall interpret the words in the light of the affectionate spirit of St. John, of whom the legend runs, that when he was too aged to enter the church, and participate in the exercises, he was, at times, brought in his chair, in order that he might bless the worshipers, and that his only expression then was, Children, love one another. Who could so well see the true unity as John, the loving, the beloved?

I. Now, he saw, leading onward, even to the consummation of the Church, the *differences* which must ever exist. He says, there are many gates to this new Jerusalem, this Church of the Future, and not one alone.

Not only are there now "several gates" into the Temple of Faith and Truth, but it was meant to be so. It is indeed very strange that men cannot become reconciled to differences of religious faith and worship—yes, even when carried out with full enthusiasm. Generally, those persons get on together most agreeably, who none of them care particularly about their individual beliefs. But surely this ought not so to be. Here we are, cast together in this planet to make the most of it, and of each other. We are made different in all respects, and necessarily led to different occupations and tastes. Well, we can easily see that sameness of feeling, taste, habit in us all would be a sad monotony; we are glad that all do not look alike, nor act alike, nor think and love alike. And yet, with strange inconsistency, the world has always been intolerant of *religious* differences; as if, when it came to the very highest department of his nature, man's whole nature were suddenly subverted, and *difference*, found divine in every other relation, here suddenly became satanic!

Now, it is easy to show that the very life of the soul, in its progressive existence, depends on these irritating differences. In the first plane, each individual is a new and different stand-point from which the universe is to be viewed. Do I wish a man to come and attempt to describe what may be seen from my own stand-point? *That* I can see better than he. I wish him to describe the view from *his own* stand-point, to which neither thou nor I, but he alone, has access.

The same may be said of churches—each is representative of some true idea, which it sees clearer than other churches. It would seem that the law of animal development, known as the "Balance of Organs," discovered by Geoffrey St. Hilaire, holds equally true of development in the religious world. The idea is, that Nature makes so much outlay of her capital on each animal, that the difference between them is one of distribution—any larger development in one part being compensated by diminution of some other. In the frog, the feet and legs have so large a claim, that the ribs are put in atrophy to allow it. In observing all the transitions, from the lizard to the serpent, we find that as the reptile grows longer, and more is needed for vertebral column, the feet are shortened, until, in the serpent, they have been absorbed altogether into the length, and the feet can only be found in their rudiments when the skin is cut. These things are properly to be stated here, because they indicate natural law, and every law runs quite through the universe. We find this balance of organs pre-eminently in our churches. Each one is as yet fragmentary—each represents some one good development which the others do not. For example, we have on one side the Universalists, who are filled with the idea of the love of God—who say that they can demonstrate all their truth from the one text, *God is Love;* these sing in perpetual sunshine. But the sunlight, though genial and sweet, contains also the deadly sunstroke. Millions of pleasant, harmless rays do indeed fall from the sun for one fell sunstroke; but still there is that terrible side to the sunlight even, which must not be ignored. So the Calvinist has a proper existence antipodal to the Universalist. He represents that true principle, which one age calls Nemesis; another, Retribution. No matter if some individuals or catechisms, not yet released from the extreme of a reaction, do overstate this idea—a wise man will easily sift all the statements of hells and devils, and see that there is a true core there, which cannot be ignored in any true apprehension of God's law. You may take any church, and shall invariably find that it has a definite reason for existence, and a principle of life, which must be an element in any future church or faith, which should be called catholic, or universal. The Romanist will affirm for you, that there must be, in the divine government, a womanly tenderness, as well as a paternal discipline; that purgation, or purification, is the prospect of the future as it is the fact of the present. The Quaker ever calls us to simplicity, and shows eternal principles in the smallest things—detecting the serpent's trail in a compliment or a dress: Methodism still utters Wesley's motto, Be in earnest: Swedenborgianism will kindle heaven at your hearthstone, and prove that the highest man must be a god. Others, which I need not name, would show, should we cut deep down into their ideas, that they too are given some stone to polish, and bring to the Holy Temple, which all must unite to rear when the true Catholic Idea shall prevail. Look around, brother; see rivers, lakes, mountains, hills, valleys, caves—dig deep enough, and you shall find the same granite rock underlying all these diversities, however various the depths.

The blunder that we make in our censure of other churches, is in seizing hold of their weakness rather than their strength. No man can help us by his weakness, but only his strength; so no church can help us by its weakness, but by its strength. It is very well, and indeed necessary, that we should recognize the differences between denominations—these differences exist to be recognized and defined, and we can only be taught all sides of the truth by seeing distinction and antagonism of ideas. The affliction is, that men will bring ugly feelings into such discussions, when every personal feeling in the sacred presence of Truth is an impertinence. If I tell the points of difference between a Calvinist and myself, I should surely take great shame if one should have reason for dreaming that I would not like that Calvinist as much as a Freethinker, or would not go as far to serve him? In any controversy, as soon as a personal feeling enters, it shows that truth is in that moment forgotten, and self, with its petty love of triumph, rises in her place. Why should I not be equally kind to a Catholic, or Calvinist, or Methodist, or Infidel, or Deist, or Atheist? I know not.

It is very certain that the churches which have best satisfied the wants of the human heart, have been those which have gone the farthest on this catholic principle, and have absorbed most of the elements of surrounding churches. A great hint was given in this direction by the rise and progress of Methodism—one which, I fear, our liberal churches are very slow to take. *There* is a church which has gone ahead, in numbers, direct influence on the masses, and general extent, of all other Protestant Churches. Why has Methodism done so much — outstripping Presbyterianism, Unitarianism, Quakerism, with their more republican form of church government? It is simply because Methodism absorbed many of the finest elements of all the surrounding churches. Its founder was the most liberal Christian of his century. That church was the child of the English Church, and retained its essential principles. To this Wesley added many of the ideas of the Moravians, with whom he was in frequent intercourse; he drew in many of the best works of the more spiritual Catholics, such as á Kempis; and he was not afraid to publish the life of the Socinian, Thomas Firmin, and recommend many of the ideas of "that good man," as he called him, to his followers. Of course, as all these churches had grown out of the wants of the human heart, the church which included the most of them was more likely to reach all classes. For you shall find, if you mingle much with men of various opinions, that what they really love in their creed is not its falsehood, but its truth; not its weakness, but its strength. Sometimes they will swallow what is false, because they have not time or ability to separate it from the truth it clings to, as its shadow; but that is not because they love it. And in any conversation with a person of another faith, if we only have the grace and sense to recognize the truth that must be, to some extent, in every creed, we shall find that they will compromise on all the rest; unless they be deacons and clergymen who, under a creed, have not, of course, their personal freedom. Perhaps no lie was ever believed. No matter how much we shudder at it, when the dogma was announced, it was a living truth to the heart which believed it, and, in higher translations and forms, the same truth shall ever be believed; and now, in *any* earnest belief, you find the exercises and signs which correspond with the highest faith. Men walked by the definite law of gravitation long before they knew that there was such a law. Men are living by the rule of the most liberal ideas, who fancy they are quite orthodox. As one said, there is a great deal of human nature in man—and the proverb, If you drive nature out at the door, she flies in at the window. All religious bitterness and intolerance shall certainly be proved one day to be a misunderstanding of one another, and churches be astonished to find that their souls have been living by a common atmosphere, as their bodies have; that their churches were spiritually lighted (though in various degrees) by the same divine sun, as the outward was by the same natural sun; that only those were totally in the dark, who thought they could imprison the light all to themselves, and so made impervious shutters all around. Ah, friends, we cannot shut up God's sunlight in any one church or house—close the shutters never so quickly, and you alone are in the dark; the sunlight fills every other temple whose doors and windows are opened wide!

II. This brings us, then, to see with St. John the principle of UNITY, which must be the basis of the Catholic

Idea. Though he saw that this holy city had several gates, there was something in common; every several gate was of one pearl. In the Oriental figures, a pearl meant PURITY. The Evangelist saw that all the various paths to God, all the different forms which Christianity, even in his day, had assumed, led upward and onward, where they were attended by purity of heart and life. No matter what their creeds, the saying of Christ must ever hold true—Blessed are the pure in heart, for they shall see God. I would say of even an atheist, whom I knew to be pure and earnest, "Brother, thou dost not yet see God, but the pure *must* see God at length." From Romanism and deadliest Calvinism, I know there often arise our Fenelons and our Edwardses; even so have I seen, from the blackest slime and mud of the river's bottom, grow up the whitest, purest pond-lilies. Indeed, were we called on to enumerate those of other churches whom we most value and love, we should not take those who stand up and comply with modern ideas, forgetting that liberality is no grace in a man who stands pledged by truth and honor to be faithful to a creed till the pledge is cast, but to those good old men who stood in terrible consistence by their faith, however horrible;* our love clings to Calvin, and Edwards, and Emmons, and Hopkins. What care we for the words they uttered? They had a pure spirit, a spirit of truth and sincerity, which, like a city set upon a hill, no cloud of false doctrine

* Decretum quidem horribile fateor.—Calvin, Ins., Lib. III, c. 23.

can hide. For each man, purity is only to be found in his own steadfast devotion to what he believes true and right. If we are not hypocrites, we shall find our Gates of Pearl; but to an unreal one, who goes each week to church, and silently avows a faith rejected by the heart, the pearly gates are discolored, and no celestial light can shine through them upon the earthly path. For purity is as much a matter of fidelity to our real creed as to anything. But no man is fit to enter the true and holy Catholic Church, who does not feel that, though the gates are several, they are all of one pearl; that pure and earnest men are always brothers; that when men unite for benevolence or philanthropy—for the right against the wrong—they enter alike the city of one God.

Very much do I fear that the source of all our dissensions is, that we are not all striving for the Gates of Pearl, but for a mere sect or self-advancement. What means this holding up of unwarranted tests of the Christian Life,—one must have just this or that in conversation and manners; "he must use words which end in *ation*," regeneration, sanctification; he must have just such and such views as are conventional about the Bible, or the personality of Jesus. But any free aspirant for the heavenly city will spurn from him all such handcuffs and fetlocks. He will say to the churches,—Brothers, so long as you demand of me purity of heart and life, you do well; you must not tolerate guilt; such toleration would root up the very subsoil from which alone Faith can grow: but when you have demanded this, your claims on me are ended; for I am free, and in all other things, stand or fall before God alone!

In fact, we can only look upon the existence of such a phrase as "religious toleration," as a biting sarcasm on the world. I should certainly look upon it as an equivocal compliment, for any one to say that I had a tolerance for all denominations,—that is, that I bore with other peoples' opinions. Tolerate indeed! You might as well say a man is good and kind because he tolerates other peoples' existence on the same planet with himself,—for a real existence includes a man's sentiments, as much as it does the room his body occupies. Tolerate forsooth! The very *a b c* of Philosophy or common sense, to say nothing of Christianity, would teach us not to *tolerate* other men's honest differences, but to *rejoice* in them,—to hold them to them,—to see that, if they are sincere and pure, their true ability to help us lies in that distinction; that for one who has eyes of his own to conform with the vision of others, would make him a mere cipher, counting only when combined with some one who was a positive figure. And are there not thousands, who in opinion are but as ciphers, added to some Calvin, or Swedenborg, or Channing, figures of positive and individual value? Let us hear the last of *toleration*. Let us *rejoice* in those who rise as new centers of thought and influence; let us as earnestly as we can *insist* that every man must enter by his own gate, that each shall have his own creed, his own worship, his own atonement, his own regeneration, his own heaven; claiming only that purity of purpose shall animate him; that each shall have the Gate of Pearl before him, within his heart the Pearl of Price.

And that this earnest spirit does animate *the mass* of every religious denomination, I must ever believe. It does seem to me incredible that men should go to the expense and trouble of building edifices, and supporting ministrations for doctrines, in their professed belief of which they are insincere. Unreal things presently die of inanition, if not at once. Much less can we believe that the expensive and inconvenient system of fasts and days with Catholics, or the "horrible" tenets of Calvinists, would or could keep any but sincere and convinced men on their rack. I know there are many in the churches who are not earnest, and have ulterior ends for compliance, but *the mass* are always genuine. It may be asked, then, why have we, if sincerity is the one thing requisite, found it necessary to discuss and oppose various forms of belief. It is because so many have *no personal faith at all.* The youth grow up and take their parents' church and creed as they live in their house. We hear human beings constantly lumped together, as if they were vegetables, to be taken in the lot,—here is a "Methodist family," and there a "Presbyterian family." Is there not room for suspicion that in such families each may not have his *own* faith, but his *father's?* If each has actually through hard thought and experience *attained* a personal faith, we have no complaint to offer, though it be Catholicism, though it be Atheism. We must sound the note which will bring every soldier to his place,—not that of parents and relatives,—but his own. When *there*, whatever his creed, he stands with the noble and true of all ages. He is one of the True Catholic Church.

Ah, my brothers, too long have we been estranged, too long forgotten Christ's prayer, "that they may be all perfect in one," not one in any such sense as would stunt the perfect development of any one; but that they may be *perfect* in *one.* Can we not have a unity consistent with individual perfection? Can we not respect the convictions and peculiarities of every earnest and pure mind, by meeting it with an equal reliance on our own peculiarities? Shall we still continue the society of the vulgar, who, in order to keep from open war, conceal their differences of opinion? Is that the way for immortal beings, who should all be equally seeking the truth, to convene? Shall men be less than dumb planets, of which we are told, "one star differeth from another star in glory?" Surely an earnest mind would suppose others equally so; a pure heart suppose others equally pure with itself.

Up over our petty dissensions, thou at least, O pure and kind heart, canst see a plane where all true pilgrims meet and rest together; a fountain, a shade, where all are refreshed alike: thou canst see those

Gates of Pearl, whose blessed light pure hearts reflect as mirrors long before they enter there!

Made in the image of one Father, children of one hope, with eyes kindled at the same spiritual sun, in the strength of a common nature, the hope of a common destiny,—join hands, knit hearts, and press on to the gates, unstained and white, through which we enter to see eye to eye, as we have loved heart to heart!

THE WORSHIPER.

And as he prayed, the fashion of his countenance was altered.

Around that man, standing on the mountain, with the splendor of God on his face, his raiment glistering in the light's flood, what momentous histories and facts cluster! See! in his single self, he represents vast primæval pains, through which nature slowly ascended from zoophyte to the human form, thus bearing in his form the progression of the world. He represents also the steadfast growth of ages, wherein this form, once gained, passed on from being a naked savage, in a paradise of sense, to being a shrine for awe and adoration; and in himself, bearing on the farthest wave, shows the line where the immortal shores are reached at last; and so up on that transfiguration mount, not alone Jesus see we, but, through him, a world looking to its magnificent future; on his heart, a race held high to catch a gleam of all it shall be when, transfigured by aspiration and worship, the fashion of its countenance is altered.

I celebrate to-day this apotheosis of all things; the central heat which causes the solid sphere to put forth wings; the light which shows the world to be on its ascent—revealing on the unfolding flower, *I ascend;* on the swelling fruit, *I ascend;* on the forming wing of the chrysalis, *I ascend;* revealing most clearly how up through man's brain and heart, lie the path and gateway whereby all things in the end enter heaven.

And this path and gateway is WORSHIP. I know the largest part of the Christian world maintain that the world is redeemed and transfigured by *Incarnation;* placing that, as a method, where we place *Worship.* They tell us that the higher descends into the lower to uplift it; that, in the conflict, God *stoops* to conquer. We trust that it is not so. We trust that the young Bettine was right when she wrote, "Nothing which is celestial passes over; but that which is earthly passes over by the celestial." The perfect can help us best by shining on there—the pure, uncompliant perfect! In God's name, let there be no descent anywhere—no incarnation; nay, no influx, but that of a spirit which, stream-like, flows on to lose itself in the all-absorbing ocean!

But that which is earthly, passes over by the celestial. Man can lift himself up to God. Up on the eternal mountains, which rise around him, he may climb till he glows in the perpetual light bathing their summits; such light not to be given to him as to a beggar, but won and claimed by him as by a hero.

And all-sufficient, indeed, is that grace which, being attained, flows from the soul to baptize all things into the holiest relations—showing that, as it was said of old, "all roads lead to Rome," there is no one thing whereon man may look or ponder, which has not its divine side, opening up a way to God.

Think it not, friend, a light thing that a man should worship, though its object be a stone, an ape, a monster. Thereby hang the tenderest, sublimest mysteries of the soul. No matter what the object is now, in every thought which is born of a sense of need, we have a *tendency* which leads to all that is highest. There stand along the pathways of the world the flaming altars; some with whiter, clearer, some with smokier, duller light; in desert caves, in monastic walls, in fanatic noisy groves, in speechless sittings, in the repetitions of Liturgies: yet remember what awful torch lighted all; remember what awful depths of spiritual need man must have fathomed, what transcendent visions of the boundless supply he must have caught; think what prelusive dreams, yearnings, phantoms, doubts, hopes, experiences must have surrounded the soul ere burst forth this sublime oratorio of prayer; think of how all that man has yet reached, all that he shall be, are implied and foreshadowed in the lowest altar ever reared!

It will be necessary for us to fix well in our minds the nature of reverence or worship, and to dismiss a great deal of cant on the subject.

In the first place, we must remember that what we have to consider is a Spirit, and not any of the specific forms it may take in any one place or period. The spirit which leads a man to doubt himself; to grope toward the mystery overlying his life; to sigh for what he knows not; to cry for help—this is spiritual worship, however much it may mistake its objects, and fasten itself to stocks and stones. What the missionary societies so pertly call idolatry, is by no means that. One earnest ray illuming their horn-eyes, would show those stocks and stones transfigured in the celestial light of the spirit, in which they are hewn and worshiped. Only the worship of Self is idolatry. The trail of the serpent is not found in the Parsee prostrate before the splendors of the rising sun, nor in the Indian low-bent as the thunder-step of God is heard in the terrible music of the storm; but in those whose prayers smack of the larder and the money-safe. We have not to go out of our own neighborhood to find the actual idolatry; all around us petitions go up for rain and crops, and physical remedies, and prosperity, from those who do not see that the Holy One, to whom they are addressed, is not really adored, but that bread and butter certainly are. The Liturgy prays that God will "preserve, for our use, the kindly fruits of the earth;" a prayer nothing different from those by which the "heathen" worshiped Ceres, goddess of crops; and one much more idolatrous, because offered after the world has been taught that God is to be "worshiped in spirit." And though under such prayers the fashion of the countenance may alter, it is to the dull gray of materialism, or the yellow of gold, not to the snow-pure luster of a spirit which cannot recall sorrow or joy of earth, in a presence before which they are as motes in the sun.

Surely it is time that we saw that the language of a pure worship would not be in the tone of one suppliant for life; would have nothing to ask; knowing that all earth's wisdom conspiring could not see our need so well as God's slightest glance; nor all its affection be so ready to give it as his most indifferent feeling; would have nothing to confess to the All-seeing; could only rejoice that God was God; could only dwell steadily on ALL THAT IS, under his rule, from atom to angel; seeking in each some lineament of the Divine Face; altering and becoming assimilated in the great brightness.

The primal fact would seem to lie somewhere in this: Man has, for all practical ends at least, a two-fold existence; one in the material, one in the spiritual world. As gravitation and other laws surround and control his body, so do spiritual laws environ his soul: they are equally definite and sure. And as man has senses to perceive, and members to obtain material benefits, so has he spiritual senses and powers to grasp and appropriate the inner and divine world.

It were a great error, however, and one to which liberal thinkers are quite prone, to suppose that worship is as simple a matter as eyesight; that a clear conscience is the open eye, which is all that we need to guide us. This natural light which is all-sufficient to distinguish right and wrong, and to secure innocence, is nevertheless as far from the spiritual height named Worship, as a lullaby is from a symphony of Beethoven's. Or, we may say, as man's eye, seeing at first the light, at length is educated into a knowledge of the spectrum, and of the relations of colors and shades, and thus refined into the highest perception of beauty and art; so the inward eye has a no less complex task; must penetrate farther and farther the depths and mysteries of spiritual life, so that mere sight shall deepen into vision and the beauty of holiness; and onward to worship, the portal perhaps to ecstacy, revealing things which, as Paul said, "it is not lawful for a man to utter."

But do not suppose that true Worship is a mere sentiment. In all of this education of it from simple sight to higher insight, the discovery is hastening on, which shows the unity of the material and the spiritual. The trained sense detects the one it has learned to love in all the atoms of his creation; ponders a divine lesson in all and each. To the holy worshiper Nanac, prostrate with his feet turned toward Mecca, there was one who cried:

"Base infidel, thy prayers repeat!
Toward Allah's house, how dar'st thou turn thy feet?"
Before the Moslem's shallow accents died,
The pious but indignant Nanac cried,
"And turn them, if thou canst, toward any spot,
Wherein the awful House of God is not."

More than all, the true worshiper has an eye quick to recognize the divine element in every *man;* by which the human relations are purified and justice secured; and in every special act where, to the coarser, no elements are working except interest or inclination, such a one sees something behind, demanding for that act a religious elevation also. In short, in reverence we recognize a great, powerful agent, which, starting from the mind in which it has been cultivated, polarizes all things in its sphere; causing all to turn toward their true star; one which thus deepens all the relations of life, lifting its Sinai, and sending forth the tables of its law in the midst of those who worship the golden calf; one which frees the intellect from the trammels of superstition and prejudice, by sanctifying its every possible object with the sense of a God dwelling in each and all; which binds every man to his right and special work on earth, by showing that to be the talisman whose charm shall lure angels and principalities to his side. Thus, beneath the pure fire of the worshiper, earth and spirit are fused into one; matter disappears, and in its place God's great Poem of Nature; man's body vanishes and, in its place, musical meanings of form and adaptation. Under this light the fashion of all is altered.

Little faith have I, for one, that any admirable work, any high success will come from any other source. The arm of might in the earth is devotion; the strength of God acts through the devout man. Can a man who looks not beyond himself and his poor dust for inspiration and strength, accomplish anything beyond what dust can accomplish? To such a one the heavens and the earth are a jest; the circling planets, a waltz; nature says, Eat and drink, for to-morrow you die. But for great action, I look to that man on whose spirit the universe rolls deep organ-tones, which call him to prayer; who has stern, unwavering faith in glorious realms, which eye cannot see, nor ear hear; who works with eye fixed steadily on an unseen pattern, given him in the Mount to copy in the plastic materials of earthly life. Such work is perfect, because worship has linked nerve and sinew on to the central power which can work no imperfection; and that worker enters the secret of him who said, "I can do nothing of myself: the Father that is in me doeth the work which ye see me do;" comprehends the sublime paradox of the earnest Paul, "I live, yet not I!"

Hence came from the experience of the world the noble and true saying, that *work is worship.* All real work is a reverence for the law and voice of God in the heart of the worker; a man's *calling*, being obedience to that which has *called* him. I know there is a kind of botching and patching of things in the world, dignified on the street with the name of work; it is only some insane men building granite and marble sepulchers for their souls; endeavoring to soothe their consumptive intellects with the prospect of coffins inlaid with gold. But every stroke of true work on the earth, breaks the spirit's chain, not forges it; each honorable coin is the seal of a man's independence, not the price for which the Lord of him is betrayed. Every fabric reared by earnest integrity and labor on earth, corresponds, stone for stone, to another which is eternal in the Heavens. And of every work we know that if it is a man's best; if it be a true worship toward his Ideal's shrine,—though before our eyes such work shall crumble to the dust ere the grass is green on the laborer's grave,—the result of that work is imperishable; on that mount of toil the soul has climbed to its transfiguration, and by every touch the fashion of its countenance was altered.

Ah, noblest indeed of all worship is work! If there is any chosen one, any darling of Heaven, it is thou, O brave man, who hast an earnest heart for work, and a strong right arm. From my lowly destiny of talker, I may at least spread the palm in the path of the noble worker, hailing him Earth's King. No Epic, whether of Homer or Dante, is like the Deed-Epic; no romance, though of Shakspere, equals the romance of the obscurest life which fills a home with the "sweet tasks of love;" no symphony can vie with the music of any life recording fulfillment in clear, strong action. Dean Swift says, "The poorest poem is better than the best criticism ever made upon it." I will say that the poorest action which is genuine, is better than the most eloquent *words about action*, which ever were or will be uttered or written.

See on the sacred mount the Son of God, full under

the glory of his Father's smile! For what, dear Saviour, art thou elect for so high preference and splendor? How art thou, from a world of men and women, singled out as the one whose tabernacle high visions of patriarchs and prophets visit, for whom God's voice breaks forth in every heart to call thee his beloved? Ah! as that weary face turns upon me, I read the sufficient answer; read it in the sharp thin lines which grief has traced upon it; read it in the scars where fearful conflicts are recorded; read it in the shadow of a cruel death already forecast on his brow. Such transfiguration did not occur on the plain of ease, but on the mount of toil; it was not given, but won. Through long vales of darkness, through the valley of the shadow of death, he came to this light: conflicts with evil, deeds of mercy, trials, labors of loneliness, these were the keen-edged prayers whereby the fashion of his countenance was altered. Never was such height attained by worship born of sentiment, and fading on the lip. And only those who die with Christ, are raised with Christ.

There is a pain which, I doubt not, we all know—a pain which comes as we remember the prayers which our childhood, with face hidden in a mother's lap, put up to one who was best known as a Heavenly Mother. How the heart filled as it repeated, one by one, the dear names which hovered about its little sphere! Not one least care was unworthy the special attention of the Maker of All. Easily, indeed, was the countenance of the child altered under *such* prayers. But then came the years which chilled them all; and if the prayers were continued, they were the merest mummies of prayers, no longer uttered with the faith and glow which once had given them wings. Sweet melody of childhood, where art thou? When I would repeat thy strain, my heart seems voiceless in every string. How often have we longed once more to bury our faces in a mother's lap, as if that had virtue to bring all back again, just as it was!

What is the matter with us? Is the soul not as dependent on its Father now as then? Are not its needs vaster—its griefs more heavy? Is it not as dear to God now? Why have such communings ceased with childhood?

It is because you have learned only the surface of that deep saying, that only by becoming little children do we enter the kingdom of heaven. We would preserve into manhood the *form*, not the *spirit*, of our childhood's trust. Such verbal petitionings are as impossible to our manhood, as it would be to preserve the old enthusiasm for the doll and the hobby-horse. It cannot be. And if we would feel the thrill and beauty of our childhood's faith again, we must be surrounded by objects as dear, and be filled with prayers as real, as those of the child. What is true to a child, is not true to a man; do not try to keep it up, or you lose the precise thing you seek — REALITY. The child asks God for temporal and personal blessings—it is natural and beautiful; the man who does it is guilty of affectation—knowing the truth, as Christ said it, "Your Heavenly Father knoweth what ye have need of before ye ask him." But the old trust, simplicity and feeling, shall re-appear in that life which utters no word or prayer which is not real and simple; which holds to the insight of manhood as it once did to the insight of childhood; which, in a word, has no attitudes to play off toward God or man, but surrenders itself unreservedly to the love and behest of truth.

More and more does it become manifest, that the question which concerns us most, concerning every man, is, Can he be counted on for strict fidelity to principle? May he be relied on for absolute allegiance to what is honorable? It is evident, that though many wish to be considered, like Cæsar's wife, above suspicion, few can be so regarded. The revolution of the wheel brings the full weight of the car on every spoke—how many have we known to snap under the pressure even when the tire is strongest!

Many things have been tried for the security of virtue under all temptations and opportunities. Wit, beauty, sentiment, feeling, learning, poetry, philosophy, each has come forth, in turn, a Dædalus to give the young Icarus wings. But the wings have melted in the sun, and the spirit fallen into the flood.

Whom, then, can we trust?

Only the man who meets God's eye everywhere and always.

Only the man whose reverent spirit makes every place or instant the focus in the whispering gallery of the universe, where all voices gather, saying, Thou, God, seest me!

Only the man whose mind, quickened by worship, detects, in the dullness or sensitiveness of his own heart, whether the heavenly smile or frown is upon him; who remembers, in every dealing, whoever be the other party, that he is dealing with God.

Only he can be fully relied on who sees the world aright; and, through the crowd of cares and affairs, is ever pressing to touch the vesture of the Most High, knowing that only when by prayer he grasps that hem, is he made every whit whole.

Up, then, O my soul! Follow on the rugged mount where the holy vision shines. Dost thou despair, seeing that transfigured one in contrast with thy heavy clay; his snow-white dazzling raiment with thy filthy rags; his altered face with thy earthliness? Despair not! Climb on, and thou too shalt be changed; for we know that we shall be like him when we shall see him as he is. Lighter and lighter each step finds the earthly about thee! Brighter and brighter on thy raiment the bleaching sun! Strive on, pray on, and over thy altered spirit thou too shalt hear, on thy transfiguration-mount, the secret whisper, This is my beloved.

THE THREE REVERENCES.

THE youngest laid their arms crosswise over their breasts, and looked cheerfully up to the sky; those of middle size held their hands on their backs, and looked smiling on the ground; the eldest stood with a frank and spirited air; their arms stretched down, they turned their heads to the right, and formed themselves into a line; whereas the others kept separate, each where he chanced to be. . . .

"Three kinds of gestures you have seen; and we inculcate a threefold reverence, which, when commingled and formed into one whole, attains its highest force and effect. The first is reverence for what is above us. That posture, the arms crossed over the breast, the look turned joyfully toward Heaven, is what we have enjoined on young children; requiring from them, thereby, a testimony that there is a God above, who images and reveals himself in parents, teachers, superiors. Then comes the second; reverence for what is under us. Those hands folded over the back, and, as it were, tied together, that down-turned, smiling look, announce that we regard the earth with attention and cheerfulness: from the bounty of the earth we are nourished: the earth affords unutterable joys. . . . Then we bid him gather courage, and turning to his comrades, range himself along with them. Now, at last, he stands forth, frank and bold; not selfishly isolated; only in combination with his equals does he front the world.

WILHELM MEISTER.

GOD

As I passed by and beheld your devotions, I found an altar with this inscription: To the Unknown God. Whom, therefore, in ignorance ye worship, him declare I unto you.

The first Reverence is for that which is above us. With minds vailed, and kneeling before the transcendent mystery and grandeur of such a subject, let our thoughts turn upon God.

It was not in haste, nor the blindness of guilt, that at Athens, the world's center of thought and culture, an altar was reared to the unknown God. We need not Paul to declare it an evidence of their superior Reverence; for it is to be observed, that the sentence rendered by our English version, "Ye men of Athens, I perceive that in all things ye are too superstitious," really should read, "I perceive that in all things ye are much given to religious devotions"—being the highest approval, and not a rebuke. Paul saw too well on what deep foundations such an altar was laid. Well did he know through what ages of speculation, doubt, inquiry, experience, the mind of Greece had climbed to that highest rung of the ladder of knowledge—the consciousness of ignorance.

It is well enough that we are brought thus to stand with Paul in Athens; for from the superior genius of the people, as well as the greater completeness of their records, we can see the natural stages by which the human mind "feels after and finds" its path through the mystery which so envelops our existence. And the human mind is one everywhere—in modern England, or New England, and in ancient Greece; as, when you have analyzed one drop of water, all oceans, seas, and rivers yield no other elements.

All speculation opens with Pantheism. Polytheism comes before it, but it is merely the first impression of the senses; Pantheism marks the entrance of real thought. It affirms that *all is God.* The faith is very old. In the Ancient Persian Parterre of Mysteries, it is taught that God is all; that each thing is only another form of the same substance, as ice, snow, vapor are different forms of water. This belief began in Greece, with her first and half-mythic poet and singer, Orpheus. At first it was the dream of poetry, and is stated in fragments attributable to him. But the dream of one age is the science of the next; and that which Orpheus sang to the music of the lyre, which he is said to have invented, was solidified in the minds of the populace as real faith. Not as the poet saw God in everything, but in a direct sense did they see him in all. Thus they ascribed to their greatest and strongest men and women the titles of God and Goddess. Hence, in Greece, Pantheism, which borders on poetry, though it remained the faith of their seers and sages, with the masses, was lost in Polytheism; and Pan, the All, shrank to a Pantheon. The Pantheistic origin of their religion is attested by the name of their highest deity, Zeus, or Jupiter. The word Zeus means *life;* the life in all was the God in all. The philosophers continued to use the names of the gods, though Hercules, Neptune, Venus, Iris, were only to them as any scientific nomenclature might be to us—meaning strength, the sea, the rainbow, beauty, and so on.

Next to the schools of the old prophets and dreamers, came upon the stage the schools of philosophy; for life comes presently to demand something more substantial than dreams and hymns. The four schools accepted Pantheism—the Epicurean, Stoic, Peripatetic, Pythagorean. It is easy to see how the consistent development of a philosophic Pantheism resulted in atheism, as it did. For if Nature was God, where was his intelligent being possible except in Man, who certainly is at the top of nature, and in whom nature becomes for the first time conscious? Then man was God; and it is manifest, that if man was the only God, there was no supreme intelligence anywhere—creation was chance, and worship, superstition.

In the reaction against this result, which presently began to be announced through their wisest men, speculation started forth in a thousand paths. And at no time could it have been better said of the Athenians, that they were "much given to religious thoughts," than when every wise man among them represented a distinct idea of God, and the earth, air, fire, water and sun were successively identified with that name as essence or symbol.

And now, thought deepens in earnestness, as the objects it had pursued are receding. There comes on Greece a period of extraordinary intellectual activity. We can imagine nothing finer than the sight which history brings into relief, upon the age of Pericles, when poets, priests, philosophers, mathematicians, orators, in that birth-place of culture, gathered together in the halls of Pericles, and quickened by the genius of the almost ideal Aspasia, sought each to find his nearest point to that Being, whom Timæus called the "circle, whose center was everywhere, whose circumference was nowhere." But beyond the definition of Socrates, beyond the dream of Plato, leaps the unclutched goal of all aspiration and speculation. The fable of the Wandering Jew, Ahasuerus, is recalled in this history of the human mind, where it was clearest and strongest, in its effort to find out God: forever seeking—never resting—it roams through all the universe which answers to faculty or sense, and at the end of every path, whence it has returned baffled and weary to press some other way, it has left its altar inscribed, To the Unknown God.

If history ended here, the student might well be a brave skeptic; and taking part with this unwearying thought against the close-kept mystery, cry, Thou Supreme Power, if indeed there be Supreme Power, why hast thou made this mind destined ever to search, never to attain? Even a man, could he make a world, would be wise and good enough to say, "Seek and ye shall find," shall be the eternal constitution of my world. But history comes nearer to only beginning here. This very vagueness and doubt were the ladder let down from heaven, whereon, to the wayworn traveler, the angels should descend. In ignorance, all true knowledge begins. And in the tone of the wiser skeptics which God sent to Greece, we see the paling of the watch-fires of human speculation before the prophetic morning-star of Bethlehem.

Homer had begun by describing God as having dark eyebrows and golden hair. And it began to appear very plainly that the most learned, who came at a much later day, though they were shocked at such physical associations with God, did nevertheless only improve it by describing, in the likeness of man, his mental and moral attributes. Let me quote a short passage from one of these satirists, who began to dissect the figure set up for adoration by the philosophic schools. Xenophanes writes:

"If beasts frame any Gods to themselves, as it is likely they do, they make them certainly such as themselves, and glorify themselves in it as we do. For why may not a goose say thus: 'All the parts of the universe I have an interest in: the earth serves me to walk upon; the sun to light me; the stars have their influence upon me; I have such an advantage by the winds, and such by the waters: there is nothing that yon heavenly roof looks upon so favorably as me. I am the darling of nature! Does not man keep, serve, and lodge me? 'Tis for me that he both sows and grinds; if he eats me, he does the same by his fellow-men, and so do I the worms that kill and devour him.' Thus the goose makes himself the end and theory of nature, and God is but the apotheosis of itself."

The graver and greater souls took the alarm, and felt that thought had now reached its impenetrable walls. Pythagoras said, "It is best we should not know God." Plato taught that the knowledge of God was the most difficult of all things, and even when attained, could not be disclosed to the masses. Socrates said, "All that I know is that I do not know."

And these were the intellectual and moral forces which in foregone ages had reared the altar *to the unknown God;* which Paul found when he came to bring Christianity to Greece.

But though all the results of thought had been one by one surrendered, their minds worked on upon the great problem. God had made it the glorious necessity of the Greek mind *to think.* Silently, deeply it plied its task.

Characteristic of the whole nation appears to me the story related of one of their most refined and cultivated minds. It was Simonides who was asked by Hiero, *Who, or what was God?* We are told that the Poet asked a day to consider; and, at the end of that, when Hiero came to get his answer, desired a day longer,—and at the end of every day, another day, saying, that the difficulty increased in exact ratio with the thought bestowed upon it. And this silent seeking, which had no answer to give, was the attitude of Greece. What in all history is sublimer than this nation, chosen for all the grand achievements of the pure intellect beyond all other nations before or since, kneeling in renunciation of all its finely wrought theories, acknowledging the stirring of wants which the intellect could awaken, but could not satisfy; but still attesting their faith in the Being who enshrouded himself from their faculties by feeding the holy flame of reverence within them, and keeping alive the fire on altars which confessed their God unknown! Blessed indeed, were those servants whom the Lord, when he came, found watching!

It was then that the voice of Paul was heard on Mars Hill, breaking the awful silence. Never elsewhere did such eager ears and anxious hearts gather around him, as when he cried, "Men of Athens! I perceive the depth and earnestness of your religious aspiration. I have witnessed your devotions, and seen your altar to the unknown God. Whom you are in acknowledged ignorance still worshiping, him declare I unto you." No voice sounding so bold a note could fail of a hearing in Athens. Admirable Paul! He did not underrate their devout spirituality,—the sinews which stood strong and ready to work; but brought the engine to which these sinews might be married, and the problem of the universe solved. He did not disparage their accumulated culture; but with the rich tissue of his inspired discourse he wove a golden thread from their own Cleanthes—"For we also are his offspring." But he declared to them that they were wasting this great religious force, in seeking to find out God as they did matters of metaphysics and science. As they went to the Agora to discuss the laws, or the grove to teach philosophy, so they went to the Temple to find out the First Cause: but, cries Paul, "He dwelleth not in temples made with hands:" he is not to be known by the mind as an object of thought. You have found that the end of this is darkness. It is well. Yet there is a reality in this mystery, a true fire at the heart of this smoke-cloud. THERE IS a great Being, the creator of us all, who hath determined all these periods of thought and knowledge among men,—so that haply they might feel after him and find him. He is not far from you. As your own poet has said, We are his children. And this was the great announcement of Christianity to the Philosophy of the World,—namely, That the Infinite God could never be an object of thought to the finite mind, but of feeling, experience; not an abstract theorem, but an inward, spiritual power.

Dwell with me an instant on this difference, and you will see what the contribution of Christianity, *as a method of search*, was to the world. You will see in the names of things true symbols of their history. The names *Theos*, *Deus*, and other words which stand for God in the ancient languages, were purely philosophic, and related to him simply as a creative force. The Egyptian Osiris is from Osireth, meaning, *the land is mine*. The Greek *Zeus* meant life; *Theos*, Creator. These words might have been addressed to electricity, if that had been discovered to be the First Cause. But Christ's word was *Father*. *That* must be addressed, not to a creative agent, but to a conscious, tender, sympathizing Being. And Christianity came to show that, not at the portal of the intellect, but at that of the devout heart, to whomsoever that knocketh it shall be opened. With *the heart* man believeth unto righteousness. God is love; whoso loveth, knoweth God. It was shown that the soul or affectional Intuition, which Stoicism had degraded as sensual, was as definitely adapted to the apprehension of the Divine Being, as the palate to food. Thus the stone that the builders had rejected, was to become the head of the corner. The phrase which had preceded Paul at Athens which pronounced Christianity *foolishness*, because it gave no new, scientific theory of the universe, he accepted boldly; "For after that," he says, "in the wisdom of God, the world by wisdom knew not God, it pleased God by the foolishness of preaching, to save them that believed."

Very grand in history, apart from all other Eras, is the Era when Christianity came face to face with Greek Philosophy. We naturally impersonate two tendencies, and see two Messiahs meeting at Athens. One was Plato, Messiah of the pure Intellect. Though dead six centuries, he comes, borne on every heart and brain in Athens, his eagle-eye flashing with the splendor of the sun of thought he is fresh from gazing on, to meet the supersolar eye of Christ, radiant with his baptism of fire. The Greek said, "I have sought him, but he cannot be found; though every ray of the sun became my torch, darkness has fallen around me." The other responds, "O Plato, not to the intellect is the vision opened: blessed are the pure in heart, for they see God." And there and then occurred the ever-glorious bridal of Plato and Jesus, the Intellect and the Soul; and whom God so joined together, no man shall ever put asunder.

I have only thought this history worthy of being related, because it is the history of every thinking man. The eagle in the embryo, is shaped like that which creeps and that which swims, ere it comes forth winged for its skyward flight. So is it with the Christian man. He must pass through all that path of vagueness, doubt, unbelief, pantheism, atheism; and then on an altar still burning within, write his own ignorance, ere he can come forth winged with Love and Faith to soar into the empyrean, whose light had blinded the eye of thought by its intensity.

Let it not be supposed that this natural history of a thinking man is supposititious. I think I can put the problem before you in such a way as to show you that the progress of Greek thought from Pantheism to the unknown God, is also your own progress, so far as you have had any. Let us try, as the human mind at first tried, to conceive of God as an object of thought,—I mean in the way in which it is constantly maintained, we may think of him, that is, through his attributes. You say, for instance, *God is infinite:* if I should now affirm he was not infinite, nothing could more shock you. But if God is infinite he must be everywhere: he must occupy every part of space: if there were any atom of which you might say, this is not a part of God, God would be limited to the extent of that atom. But what else is this than Pantheism? This wood must be God if he is everywhere. We ourselves must be God, if that is so. The same result comes of any other attribute that the intellect may ascribe to him. Take that of Omnipotence, for example. If God is Almighty, all power is derived from him: you cannot conceive of an act independent of his strength; whether it be the gift of charity, or the plunge of the assassin's dagger. He does all, and so moral distinctions are lost.

But do you then deny that God is infinite and omnipotent? No more than I mean to deny that there are beings in the planet Neptune, who have wings and twelve eyes. I only mean that for the intellect to make such affirmations, is as foolish as for a man to close his eyes and turn his ear to a painting to discern its merit,—the intellect being related to God, only as the ear to the picture. I have only designed to show you that the intellect without the heart is an atheist. And people are none the less atheists when they have a number of canting terms on their lips about God and his attributes. That is worse than silence.

It is heart-worship, then, that reaches God; not intellectual acumen. And this reverence is based on love. By the training of life through affection, love is ever seated on the throne in man, ideally, if not actually, and through it comes every conception of what is the highest good. It is therefore true that "we love Him, because he first loved us;" not because that appealed to our self-love, but because it showed him to be a loveable being. This is the law of love. It is as the rain falls easiest where the ground is already wet; is as only something magnetic attracts the loadstone,—a piece of wood will not. We cannot love an abstraction, nor a set of laws; nor can be touched by a mere historical or arbitrary relation to God. The heart is that Cordelia whose filial love cannot come forth by threats or rewards, but, knowing its sacred laws, responds to whatever claims its affection, as she to Lear:

> I cannot heave
> My heart into my mouth; I love your majesty
> According to my bond; no more, no less.

A child does not revere a *mere parent;* but the tenderness, affection, and goodness implied in the word parent. Were these absent, physical relationship could not secure it. On the other hand, the love of what is lovely is unavoidable, if there be no perversion of the natural action of the emotions.

How cruel a wrong to the heart and its most sensitive feelings, how cruel a wrong to its upward strivings, is done by those who give it a God who does violence to its instincts! The very spring of the divine life is tampered with! Men may call infinite wrath, scathing with hell's lightnings myriads of souls; infinite injustice, heaping on one innocent soul the punishment of a world's sin; infinite caprice, electing some, reprobating others—men may *call* these God; then the soul *knows* that, in her highest condition, she cannot love nor worship such a God; cannot love wrath, caprice, injustice; as if through the world a law should be proclaimed, making dishonesty the legal duty of every citizen, and the scaffold the reward of honesty, we should soon have communities springing up, who would sanctify the scaffold by dying on it, honest men. We may have doubt concerning many doctrines—of this one we are certain: God is Father of our spirits;

it is He that hath made us: and if we are so constituted as to love what is lovely, and hate what is hateful, it is His work; and if, for not accepting as our God a tyrant, governing only by threat or bribe, we shall be sent to hell, we know that the truest souls shall be there—souls that staked all on love and justice—souls whose companionship were far better than any God who would send them there—

> For a loving worm within its sod,
> Were diviner than a loveless God
> Amid his worlds!

Far inward, then, to the shrine of the heart's sacred ideal of all that is fair and dear—where the cold questions of logic cannot penetrate, where the rude hand of fanatic dogmatism cannot lay waste its altar—let the human spirit repair to meet its best-beloved. And shall the intellect share nothing in the sacred joy? Surely God hath no angel so beautiful as the intellect, which, having found its sweet ignorance, obeys gladly the soul's wand. Upward and ever upward let it soar! And as, uplifted upon it, we rise to height above height of nature, probing the immensities which overlie and underlie us, the soul's upturned eye answers the smile of God, which illumines all: "Thou Great Being, whom I cannot name—here, 'where worlds on worlds eternal brood,' where thought grows faint before the stupendous vista—my heart whispers, and its whisper I will trust—Surely the Power is but a drop in the Ocean of Love."

Brothers, can we ever forget the joy when this faith entered? O, the stumbling on the dark mountains! when Reason went forth over the great deeps, and, like the dove, returned bearing no leaf of promised rest; when the brain was racked with doubt, and the flesh fainted, because they said, Where is thy God? The universe was silent. When the hard face of atheism was turning the heart to stone; when the cry was already rising from flower, bird, man, *Fatherless!*—hark the angelic voice, Stay thy hand! And another eye, the eye of a loving heart, opened, as the mind's eye closed in weariness. Then felt we pulses of Eternal Love; for the first time knew we the full meaning of FATHER.

NATURE.

And if thou wilt make me an altar of stone, thou shalt not build it of hewn stone; for if thou lift up thy tool upon it, thou hast polluted it.

So early in the history of our race was the first reverence connected with the second—reverence for God, who is above us, with reverence for Nature, which is beneath us, yet which He made, and saw that it was very good. The altar built of simple natural stone, unhewn by man's workmanship, symbolizes well enough the truth, that Nature is a temple for worship, and that our earth, just as God has made it, is the altar whereon the spirit's highest devotions may be offered; and thus is itself to be revered, from daisy to world, as every whit holy.

It is well that the reverence for what is above is said to precede the reverence for what is beneath us; for it is only in this light that Nature can be really seen at all. It is fashionable, I know, to pay a kind of lip-service to Nature, her fine days, and most peculiar phenomena. But he alone really sees Nature who sees God in it; to whom every grass-blade is a letter signed and sealed by the Supreme Love; in whom a devout eye has secured such harmony with it, that the spirit reflects the simplicity and freedom, bloom and grandeur of Nature in adequate life and action. None ever saw a sunbeam to whom it was not a love-glance from heaven. None ever saw the sky to whom it was not the Father's blue eye, full of peaceful benediction. And no astronomer ever saw more deeply than the child, who thought the stars small holes to let the glory through. Each one is just that; and to the childlike, all things share the illumination.

A poet has written:

> 'T is heaven alone that is given away—
> 'T is only God may be had for the asking;
> There is no price set on the lavish summer,
> And June may be had by the poorest comer.

I cannot quite respond to this. I am constrained to think that within and beneath every fair object in Nature, there lurks treasure which only a life of patience, trial and virtue can win. The Nature which shines in upon the eye, or stirs the membrane of the ear, is cheap enough; but how small a part is that! But let me not anticipate.

I. Nature first enters man through the doorways of sense. The religion of the senses is utilitarian. Their perception of the world is as a store-house of bounties. They are willing enough to acknowledge a being who gave these bounties, but care not to look beyond their benefit to the senses. Their highest name for that being is *Providence*. And this is well; for it promises the highest spiritual relations to Nature at last, as a fish's fin promises a man's arm. There is a wise Oriental proverb, which says, "With patience and labor, the mulberry-leaf is changed into satin." Man, like the cocoon, fastens himself on the world through his senses; but this is the beginning of an ascent; for soon after Nature enters sense, she becomes an object of

II. The intellect. He experiences that all things tend to educate him. Where he was a huntsman, he now becomes a zoologist; where he was a plowman, he now becomes a naturalist; finding that animals and plants are not alone good to be eaten, but have certain habits and appearances which the intellect has an interest to examine. He visits the fields without gun, and the brook without rod. The senses found in Nature their nurse; the intellect finds in her a school-dame. What discipline is in the observation of natural objects and facts; what economy of time and labor we learn in the directness with which a stone falls to the ground, and the general precision of all things; what lessons of means and ends in the adaptation everywhere seen — the humming-bird's beak fitted to the honeysuckle's urn of sweets, the wading-birds suited with long legs, and the grazing animals with long necks; what inculcations of individual purpose in the steadfast isolation of all things; so that, under no circumstances, can ice and fire do each other's work, nor lead and iron be interchangeable in offices! All these are to the faculties of the mind what the gymnasium is to the limbs of the body.

And thus far mankind have penetrated Nature, and are at home. Indeed, the faith which men have in Nature, is one of the most beautiful sides of life. A little block of wood, which, in former years, a surveyor's axe has marked, will, before a jury, convict a million men of perjury, ere the mute testimony of its growths shall be doubted. No man could ever conceive of a lie in tree or flower.

III. But now commences the transition into an equally positive but more difficult sphere. Whatever King Midas touched, was turned to gold, says the fable; but Midas could not live on gold, and so perished with the bread changed to gold in his hand. The intellect does, indeed, transmute the objects of sense into the golden laws of science, but it leaves a craving going on unsatisfied. That does not supply the whole man which feeds the body and the intellect; man is more than body and intellect. "It is written, man shall not live by bread alone, but by every word that proceedeth out of the mouth of God." It is needful that some power shall quicken each object into a word from God's mouth, ere man realizes the full meaning and joy of the universe, in which it is appointed him to dwell.

Carefully let us pick our way here—seeking for truths, not fancies.

The highest point gained is the perception of a Soul in Nature; and this perception begins its formation through the presence of beauty everywhere around us. The faculty which responds to this sacred baptism of the universe in loveliness, is not exactly the intellect, nor the religious soul, but partly both, and is properly called *Taste*. A cultivated taste perceives that in Nature beauty is omnipresent; for there is no object in Nature which sufficient light will not make beautiful. Some one has remarked, that under an intense light, a decaying corpse has the most transcendent and heavenly beauty. And this all-pervading element, which is only designed as a lure to something deeper than itself, brings on a train of thought which presently startles man, as by a supernatural presence. For he reflects that there is beauty beyond the reach of his eye. In vast coral-beads, and forms of aquatic life, under the sea; in close-closeted pearls; in unmined diamonds; in polar glaciers, and desert flowers—there are realms of beauty, which the eye of man can never see. Early strata and caves attest that beauty was glowing in the world thousands of years before the human eye was created. Why should these things have been made beautiful? If beauty answers a definite end, how was it served when it stretched out beneath the eyes of reptiles and fishes?

Reason whispers that it was not wasted; that there was no ray of this divine beauty which did not shine on some eye, and light up some spiritual star. And man is brought to question if there be not something deeper than he may have thought, in that which he terms so hastily the *instinct* of the orders of nature, which are beneath him. I would acknowledge the mystery of nature, nor fail in caution where the line between reason and speculation is so slender; but the knight of the olden time read on three sides of the temple, *Be bold*,—on one, *Be not too bold.* Even the caution need not stay our entrance, where the torches which guide us are the definite facts of natural history, and the path clear induction.

The first fact which meets us is our inability to define how far sensitive life descends into the creation, from man downward. We know that animals not only have sensation, but are individual in mind or instinct, (or whatever you may choose to call that for which we have no name). An individual is a unit. Now, when we take one of the lower forms of life, such as the sponge, we find that, in one individual, both animal and vegetable life are developed. The sponge grows as a vegetable, and when it is torn from its rock it writhes with evident pain until it is dead. But since it is a unit, we must ascribe this susceptibility to pain to the vegetable as well as the animal. Well, if you can predicate sensation of any one vegetable, you cannot tell how far it descends; but it may be supposed far beyond our ability to discern. As far it may be as life itself,—which is found even in the mineral kingdom, for any stone-mason shall tell you the difference between live rock and dead rock. These are our kindred, since we have life in common. The botanist when asked, Why does the sensitive plant shrink? replies, It is not known, but the best theory is that it has something like a nervous system. Milk is found healthy for many plants, as the cocoa, as well as for animals; and the chemists tell us there is far less elementary difference than was imagined, between the sap of plants and the blood of men.

With equal reason we may say, that as we cannot fix the limit of the susceptibility to pleasure and pain in creation, and might, if our eyes were keen enough, detect its fainter manifestations in the granite hewn from its bed, so neither can we affix a limit for the *spiritual* element. As the inferior animals answer bone for bone, sense for sense, to our physical frame, how do we know but that, if we could penetrate all that is inclosed in the term "instinct," we should discover the germs of an organic, intellectual existence? The phenomena of the instincts of plants and animals, which amuse our earlier days, are entitled to a far more serious thought now. Almost all naturalists concede the moral nature of animals; finding in them hope, fear, love, and, in many instances, a plain knowledge of right and wrong.

Then the moralist enters with his testimony, and asks, Why is all this suffering in the world? It is against the belief in a good God, to suppose that there can be a single pang in the world, except for moral uses and ends. Suffering is for benefit. Yet here we find that not only is there suffering throughout the animal creation, but the vegetable is not exempt,—the mimosa, the sea-plants, suffer pain. Only cruelty could have ordained pain where there is no higher life to need its discipline! But, if there be in all these lower orders a faint, spiritual essence, which has its consciousness and flowering in man alone, then we know what upward strivings result from the universal suffering; and we know, too, the uses of the universal beauty, even where it shines on the eyes of the inferior, animated world alone. There is a divine element of which this beauty is at once the sign and discipline. And we stand fairly in the presence of the sublime fact that life,—divine and beautiful LIFE,—saturates and glorifies the universe. The voice cries, as of old, "Do NOT I FILL ALL THINGS, saith the Lord?" Then does man enter the universe with holy awe,—for wherever the spiritual element is, God is; and this calls forth the reverence for what is beneath us. In this light Solomon, in all his glory, may sit at the feet of the lily. Every step is on hallowed ground. Each atom of the fair world, however lowly to the vulgar, to the devout spirit rises to be a polished pillar in

> That Cathedral boundless as our wonder,
> Whose quenchless lamps the moon and stars supply;
> Its choir the winds and waves; its organ, thunder,
> Its dome the sky.

My brothers, thus I say to myself: As life goes on,

and the one thing in any moment unchanged, is change itself; as empires rise on the great flowing, ebbing sea of Time, to burst, bubble-like, in a moment; as wrong, falsehood, hypocrisy, gnaw like worms at the heart of the Tree of Life; as men fight and devour one another for perishing toys, such as gold or thrones,—one thing will the true soul claim which includes them all, *Nature.* An old traveler found in a barbarous tribe, one woman set apart from others who maintained that she was affianced to the sun; what cared she for the poor maggots around her, what, for the roar of the distant worlds of civilization,—was there one object of the earth which was not kept alive, or brought to its perfection, or clothed with beauty from the magnificence of her Beloved One? Where, cries the spirit, is the light that bathes all—which is as glorious on ruins as on palaces—which floods all things small and great with splendor,—thither, O thither, will I press to my beloved! Heaven shall be his smile of light! Hell shall be the cloud which vails his face from me! Not face to face can the spirit meet her sun with its terrible brilliance; but in all fair forms of nature he is reflected; and in the love and reverence of nature she finds her Lord.

Nature never did betray
The heart that loved her. 'T is her privilege
Through all the years of this our life, to lead
From joy to joy; for she can so inform
The mind that is within us, so impress
With quietness and beauty, and so feed

With lofty thoughts, that neither evil tongues,
Rash judgments, nor the sneers of selfish men,
Nor greetings where no kindness is, nor all
The dreary intercourse of common life
Shall e'er prevail against us, or disturb
Our cheerful faith that all that we behold
Is full of blessings!

In all that is called social progress, formation of character, and spiritual insight, we shall find the essential element to be an advance toward a realization of and harmony with Nature. Suppose the social Utopias were all realized in any community; all being at work in their true places; none idle, and none poor; each protected and guarded by all the rest—nothing would be gained beyond what exists in any bee-hive, or coral-bed. What is the essence of what we call *Character* in this world? It is simply unswerving self-reliance. The superior men of this world are those who find the bent and power of their own nature, and rest upon that. For the inclinations of our minds, for certain special callings, is Nature welling up in us, as truly as a spring bursting up is Nature. The old mottoes of the great—Know thyself, Obey thy heart—are but calls for us to enter the sacred circle of things which are strong and beautiful, by being what God meant them to be. Plato is a philosopher exactly on the principle that sugar is sweet; Shakspere is a poet as a diamond is bright. The differences of human character may be easily reduced to the question, Which is truest to

Nature? of beauty, which is most natural? of manners, which is freest from affectation, or a disguise of Nature? This is the test of all, corresponding to the Litmus of chemists, by which they detect the presence of acids anywhere. No circumstances can cover up the law. A throne cannot hide the meanness of a natural butcher, as Caligula, perverted into a king—while Diogenes, following his nature into a tub, plants the seed of greater and nobler systems of faith and philosophy.

And as it is social progress, and personal character, so is it the law of *spiritual insight.* It would be amusing, if it were not of a deeper interest, to see the slow iconoclasm of Nature amidst the most venerable systems of the world. No sooner has the Sabbatarian proved his point, and draped the world for one day of the seven in a dingy puritanic pall, than some un-calvinistic bird comes twitting and laughing down the whole arrangement, and grasshoppers, bees and fishes cannot be frowned into suspending their Sunday merriment. People are not so certain about the Sabbath; but they *know* that God made the bird, and did *not* make it more gloomy on one day than another. And so with many human creeds: Nature is too much for them. Men may talk of fire and brimstone; but when we find that there is no beast of prey which does not destroy its victim in the least painful manner possible, we know that there shall never be in the universe one superfluous pang—not one day of suffering for any soul beyond what is best for all. I want no argument weightier than a rose or a sunbeam, to dispel all the dark shadows which superstition and dogmatism have cast on the face of our loving God. While, on the other hand, every object in the earth and sky is a tongue of flame to attest the reality; no flower is there but preaches, in every stage of its growth, the true regeneration; no pendent calyx, but is a bell calling to orison and vesper; no grass-blade, but is a church-spire, pointing upward to the Infinite Love, to whom the universe ever turns as a flower expanding toward the sun.

And, to be felt and trusted, our Faith must be put forth from our hearts as naturally as the grass and grain are put forth from the heart of the earth. Whence this complaint of the apathy of the world to the Church? The grass does not complain that the herd will not feed upon it. And when the church-altar is built of simple stones, without the polluting handicraft of priests and councils lifted upon them, to shape them for their own sectarian edifices, men will bring their heart's blood, if need be, to pour out as libations upon that altar to the God, by whom and for whom the heart's blood of all men really beats at last.

If the Romanist may, on each Christmas eve, have his great St. Peter's Cathedral flash forth suddenly, by its annual miracle, with dazzling light from every window; the great dome rising up like a heaven of fires; each turret leaping to a spire of flame, causing the worshiping throng to fall prostrate beneath heaven's fire-flood—surely we who have chosen to worship in Nature as our temple, may treasure up the moments when God, with ineffable glory, fills and overflows the world. Thou art my friend—I am thine; so may I remember here, how out of a corrupt, heartless city, where Satan held a steady scepter; out from the cries of those who, in street and church, set up their idol, and cried, O Baal, hear us! out, out I pressed, weary, heartsick for a breath of truth, to the woods and fields. Up the steep hill-side I climbed, leaving all the garish city behind—sick and tired of it, I say! The fiery streaks of approaching day flecked the east; and presently the first golden glance of the day's eye smote me. I turned, and O! what did I see? Over against the sun stood a great elm, which might have grown a century for the glory of that day; through it the stream of light flowed into my heart; each stately branch, a pillar of fire; each leaf, a pentecostal flame-tongue. Then I knew how Moses came down from the mount, with face flushed with the glow of the burning bush; when God met him in the bush which burned, and was not consumed. Here it was again, kindled for my morning-prayer. Then I knew God was near—in sound of my voice. My soul cried, O my Father! it is good to be here; and here let thy love rear a tabernacle, where thou shalt dwell with me, and never, never remove.

Then out from the glory of the burning bush came a voice, to which all Nature chanted chorus—Thou, poor child, whose dust dilates beneath the Infinite Love, sped with every sunray, thou standest in the Church of the first-born. Here is the temple into which the ransomed of the Lord shall come with songs, and everlasting joy upon their heads—NATURE. Men have imitated the trunks of these trees in the pillars of their cathedrals; the lofty embrace of their branches have copied in the arches of their fretted ceilings; they have travestied the piping winds and the songs of birds in their organs. It is well; but they are thus only trained for a purer communion, face to face, with the spirit of Nature, which, when it shall shine on man's simple surrendered spirit, shall bring him to a grandeur but faintly hinted in this great sunrise, whose elements of mere mist and light are far cheaper than those of his wondrous nature!

MAN.

WHEN I consider thy heavens, the work of thy fingers; the moon and the stars which thou hast ordained; What is man, that thou art mindful of him and the son of man, that thou visitest him? For thou hast made him a little lower than the angels, and hast crowned him with glory and honor.

IN every land poetry has gained its greatest rapture when it has celebrated man. Here the superior soul is enlisted, and the tongue of flame descends. In man is the marriage of heaven and earth, and all things gladly unite in chorus to celebrate the holy and sublime sacrament.

The poet and king of Israel went forth to commune with God in nature: but in himself he found both,—nature was transfigured in his thought, and the godlike soul arose. The pomp and glitter of the Court which he had left, faded under this high illumination. The greatest crown of the East whose gems shone on his forehead, was forgotten as tinsel. On his brow was pressed the coronet of a more royal dignity,—his crown as a MAN. God had made him a little lower than the angels, and crowned him with glory and honor!

Surely nothing can be finer than this inspiration which saw, nay felt, the meeting of God and nature in man, as sea meets shore. The Psalmist thinks of the heavens as the work of God's fingers, the moon and stars as what he has ordained; blending thus the first and second reverences,—reverence for God and for nature, as his expression; but the fact that he, by virtue of his manhood, stands there as the rivet of the two, bearing in himself both God and nature, leads him to the last, but not least reverence,—that for what is around him; for those who stand on the same plane of the universe with himself; for man.

What a vast and varied labyrinth of phantoms, struggles, dreams, doubts, hopes, fears, does man enter when once he rends the vail of consciousness, and seeks to tread the hidden paths of his own nature!

Although the highest wisdom of all nations has warned us of the dangers of a life from without, and heroic voyagers of the inward seas have told of the mystic splendors there, and the pearls of price far hidden in the soul's depths; although philosophy, from the first, has written on her temple-front, *Know thyself*, and the oracles of religion cried, *Commune with thine own heart;* yet mankind have always had a dread of knowing too much about themselves. Anatomy, as a science, has fewer lovers than any other; and phrenology, physiognomy, and other systems which aim at perception of personal character, are staved off almost fiercely, while others with half their evidence are received with little question. There is something sublime in this shudder with which man approaches the Ark, even where he is the anointed Priest. For this awe of knowledge has never been felt except in the sublimest realms. Faust sold to the Arch-fiend, and Prometheus bound as the eternal prey of the vulture, are national fables which testify the fear which guarded a knowledge of the secret things of God and Nature. The fable of the eating of the fruit, which revealed the knowledge of his own good and evil, shows man's shudder at penetrating his own mysterious Self. These are the grandest continents of the spiritual sphere which is within us. And I would that with this awe heightened into reverent earnestness we should approach the subject of *man*,—man, to whom has been assigned every seat in the universe, from the floor of the pit to the throne of a God; man, whom Rochefoucauld will show with plausibility and wit to be a bundle of selfish passions, while Paul cries, "Know ye not that ye are the Temple of God?"

There are two tones in the verse I have quoted, which it is well to observe, as we shall find, perhaps, that they correspond with two tones which may be heard in man himself. What is man, that thou art mindful of him? This tone is disparaging; yet let us follow it, for it is a true note, and the truth will always be found most beautiful in the end.

I. Man, then, is an animal. There is no essential difference that can be pointed out between him and the inferior orders. The naturalist tells us that he has a thumb to his hand where the animals with hands have fingers only; or that his skull sits on the top of the vertebral column, where even the ourang-outang has it thrust forward. But these are only enough to show him another, doubtless a higher, variety of animal. It is not contended that there is a joint, or fibre, or sense, or function of blood and nerve in man which is not in the quadruped also. The lower animals also dance, sing, love, hate; are fond of music, are fond of dress; they build, sew, plant, weave,—and pursued these things long before man, who, the ancient writers say, learned these arts from them. I would that the identity ended here, but it does not. It is in vain for us to assume that with the beginning of the reign of man on earth, the reign of the animal ceased. Not so, my masters! One could almost fancy that when man was about to be created there was a rumor of it among the lower animals; and that they, dissatisfied with their more constrained forms, collected about the centers where man was to appear, and as the upright forms arose, climbed into their hearts and brains. So that, despite the erect posture, one man became an ape, another a bear; some were snakes in the grass, some foxes, some wildcats; many donkeys. They have only told half the fact, who have found physical resemblances in men to certain animals. The dispositions are preserved as well. Society frequently presents the appearance of a menagerie of fierce, sly, proud, and stupid animals. It is even worse in him,—for the *bona fide* animal may be kept in the barn-yard on account of his form; but what defense is there against the two-footed calf or mule that may bring his hoofs in at your front door?

I am serious in what I say. I mean that in every government, congress, or parliament; in every fashionable assembly, you will hear the bray of asses, the hissing of geese and serpents; that war dates from the beasts of prey, and slavery is a relic of the hyena.

II. But, though this is the truth, it is not the whole truth concerning our nature. To stop on our animal nature, and say, *Behold the human heart*, is the common way with theologians; but it is as if you should at night point a man's eye to the earth and say, *Behold the planetary universe;* nor regard the heaven of fires which vaults above that earth. Thus, though the first note is low, the moon and stars which he has ordained to rise above man's earthliness, the heavenly lights of the soul which are jewels to crown him with glory and honor, enable us to strike, with the poet, a nobler key; Thou hast made him a little lower than the angels, and hast crowned him with glory and honor! We cast the glove to the misanthropist. Does he charge crimes? We will answer with heroisms: does he point to prisons? We will point to temples and asylums: does he bring science to prove man another link in the animal chain? We will respond with the higher science which proves that in him the link fastens on to angels and archangels. In harmony with this high claim, we find the definitions of man which the race has formed in its highest moments and localities. The Greek word for man was ανθρωπος; a word formed of three others (ανω, τρεπο, οπς) signifying *to turn the eye upward*. Man worships the unseen and eternal. His eye overleaps the foregrounds of life, which hem in the animal sense, and claims the horizon as a portal to the house not made with hands, eternal in the heavens. In all nations this higher realm of our nature has been recognized; but in none more truly than the Oriental, who affirm that the animals traveled through a thousand forms toward the spiritual world, rising step by step from the prostrate worm upward; but at their highest they could only wander on the shore of the great gulf, which separates the earthly from the heavenly. Then was man created as the bridge, to leap that chasm, whereon all that was animal might pass over to the spirit; for he rested with his body on the shore of the animal, but with his soul on the shore of the spiritual. And by him all things ascend.

I will venture here and now to give full and hearty consent to this ancient faith. It is too common for us to pass without notice, the fact that our expressions for natural facts, and for personal facts, are synonymous; that we speak of the *face* of nature, the *veins* of metal, the *bowels* of the earth; that light and darkness, warmth and coldness, are as much expressions of mental conditions, as of physical facts. We are content to enjoy the blessings of nature, without asking why it is that every animal, mineral, and vegetable, strives to feed, and clothe, and heal, or in some way bless us. Surely it is because the whole creation is garnered and reproduced in man. The vegetable grows in his hair, the mineral in his bone, the metal in his blood, and, as we have seen, the whole animal kingdom in his organs of sense. Thus related to all, all may enter him and be translated into thought and emotion,—for he is the bridge over the chasm. There is not a weed or poison but through some botanist or chemist will become eloquent and philanthropic; no insect, stone, star, but is humanized, and rises to poetry and spirituality. Man is, indeed, as Paul said, the Temple of God; and in him nature comes to kneel and adore. This ascent begins with his own body, which is nature in quintessence. Through his genius the body radiates higher mechanic forces; the lever is modeled from his arm; the hammer is his fist in iron; his finger is lengthened in a rope; his hand is copied in all pronged instruments; his head-curve is the plan of the stone arch; his body the original of his house. Then nature beyond is reached. Through his genius and spirituality heavy granite and limestone rise to sing and pray in the Cathedral, which Coleridge called a "petrified religion;" his pencil gives spirituality to bogs, swamps, decayed trees; the rough marble breathes with an ideality which man himself cannot reach. The absorption and apotheosis goes on in the higher spheres of nature. The mental structure projects itself in governmental forms; its threefold division, into the Intellect, the Sensibilities and the Will is repeated in the Executive, Judicial, and Legislative departments; which, more or less perfectly, are found in even the rudest governments. Creeds, Churches, Angels, Gods, are celestial copies of the human model. Man's progress is simply more entrance of nature into him, and freer passage to the spiritual shore. By him all things exist, and without him nothing is made that is made. Without his brain nature is a huge mud-ball; without his eye sunrises were but damp fogs. "We know (says Paul) that the whole creation groaneth and travaileth in pain, awaiting deliverance into the glorious liberty of the children of God."

The thought that man, whose nature we bear, is here as the center of the physical universe, and God's highest word thereto; nay, his grapple fixed thereon to raise it to his own beatitude, fills me with an awe akin to terror! Before him nature fades, as a frame before the portrait it surrounds. Sinai shrinks to a hillock when Moses stands upon it. What is Thermopylae when Leonidas is there? What ant-heaps are the seven hills of Rome when Cicero's voice is heard!

We have spoken of the two other reverences; for what is above us,—for what is beneath us. It is now to be stated that both of these cease to be theoretical, and become practical and vital only when they concern reverence for man. For we know nothing of God, save as he stirs and inspires the soul of man; nothing of nature, except as interpreted by the brain of man. Life among men is the practical test of what reverence we have for what is above and beneath.

For God is represented on earth by the best men. These are they who hold more of the celestial light than others; who by a closer intimacy with nature, more answering harmony with the laws of their being, and a stricter surrender to their own vital force, are elect for superior offices. They are giants and kings among men. When God sends such into his vineyard, he says, "They will reverence my sons." The first, reverence for God, is involved here: they speak and act for God; His honor is bound up with theirs. But how true is the parable! How have men in every age stoned and rejected those thus sent. See all along the highways the hemlock, the scaffold, the block! Hear on every wind the cry of the multitude, "Crucify him! Give us Barabbas, the thief, instead of him!" What else is said of our best teachers and reformers to-day? Are they our presidents, kings, judges, and representatives, as they would be if we bowed beneath the scepter of the God for whom they stand?

And, on the other hand, reverence for what is beneath us never rises to its sacred summit until it is called for by our relation toward the weak, poor and ignorant. Here reverence for the lower ceases to be sentiment. Of all things the most difficult is properly to estimate and respect those who are our inferiors.

As it is easy for the weak to cling to the strong, it is hard for the strong to respect the weak. Yet nothing would better indicate the advance of civilization. The savage despises weakness; will slay a child because it cries, or a woman because she faints. Our civilization shows the old savage instinct when it turns from the drunkard and the harlot; when it justifies or ignores the enslavement of millions because they are of an inferior race, that being the truest seal to their claim on our help and protection. In the first age men will eat each other. In the next this ceases, but they will slay and rob each other. The next will abolish this, but replace it with war and slavery. We await the age which shall cease these also, and realize the full sadness of the fact, that this poor humanity so despised, maltreated, slain, enslaved from age to age, is God's own heart; shall see in each who is wronged the bleeding Christ, and hear him say again, "What ye have done to the least of these, my brothers, ye have done to me."

The least of these his brothers! Can it be that each man we see, of whatever degree or complexion, has in him that immortal flame which certifies his brotherhood to the Son of God! Has each the wondrous soul which is little lower than the angels!

O my poor, bleeding Christ, I cannot hide from thee! Thou meetest me on the street each day of my life meekly bearing thy five red wounds, in those the least of whom cannot be wounded, but thou art wounded.

There in the hovels are the children, growing up in ignorance and vice, whom our free and Christian State decides shall not go to our schools, because they are not white. Ah, how plainly I saw, each little hand had the mark of a bloody nail in the center! This week I met thee again. Against all law, and all right, three helpless ones were sent away into bondage,—two of them infants, not dreaming of the fearful fate awaiting,—by a thing called a judge; our miserable, venal press, with one exception, applauding; and the community going on heedless of a wrong, which, in our midst, crucified our Lord afresh!

My friends, I ask no pardon for speaking of these things here. Rather pardon us, thou spirit of humanity, that we go on in our apathy and self-seeking; and, seeing thee there, fallen among thieves who have left thee wounded and stript of all thou hadst, have passed by on the other side! But if we have forgotten those who are weak and wronged, God has not; and their cry shall pierce where the saintly prayer which forgets them shall fail to enter. Whoso touches one of those little ones, toucheth God's heart; whoso forgets them and their claim, hath forgotten their Infinite Father. Better were it for that man that a millstone were hanged about his neck, and he cast into the sea. God is as mindful as you, ye mothers, of his children, made in his image. "Can a woman forget her sucking child, that she should not have compassion on the son of her womb? Yea, she may forget; yet will I not forget thee!"

The present organization of society cannot last; the world is even now budding in every branch and twig with revolution. And why? Because the world is organized on the basis of *contempt for man.* O ye lords! O ye ladies! Your East Indian delicacies are rich and rare. Feast, adorn yourselves, be merry! What elegant forms Indian sinews assume as they reach you,—golden, superb! Let the swarthy fellows work on! What affair is it of yours if India is a galley-slave, her fair land a brothel for your fine East India Company! Hark! what cry is that? Why do you turn pale?

> "Suddenly out of its stale and drowsy lair,—the lair of slaves,
> Like lightning Delhi leaps forth,—half startled
> At itself; its feet upon the ashes and the rags;
> Its hands tight to the throats of tyrants."

What means this crash of trade? It means that man is trifling with man. It means that in Wall Street, in State Street, men are gambling with the coined heart's-blood and sinews of labor; gambling where the very bread of the widow and the orphan is the stake. Trade, too, it would seem, is based on the contempt of man; men looking on others much in the light of sheep, valuable chiefly on account of their susceptibility of being fleeced.

I say again, that the present organization of society is on a foundation of sand, and cannot last.

And for all the dreary catalogue of crimes against man, not any one man, or country, or section, is to be arraigned. More than any other, I take shame in saying it, the so-called Church of Christ on earth is to be arraigned. Has it not trained men from their infancy to despise and detest their own nature? Has it not taught that every man, even in childhood, is to be distrusted? Has it not taught that God holds men so cheap, that the mass of them are to be damned everlastingly; and that those who are not, are to be saved by all manner of crouchings, whinings, and supplications, like spared slaves? What wonder if men despoil, crush, rob, and enslave this child of the devil; this walking leprosy; this alien and outcast? Does not God feel that way toward him? Is he not angry with him every day? I do not wonder that the great church-bodies all over the world, are on the side of oppression. No man can estimate the lashes, the chains which Dogma has imposed on humanity,—binding both body and soul.

I arraign no less our liberal or free Christianity, as we complacently call it. I fear that with the majority of us, the binding of a slave is not so horrible as the doubting of a miracle. Our Boston Unitarians will commune with slaveholders, but not with Theodore Parker,—that brave, true man, who stands now with broken health, yet where he ever stood in front of the phalanx of God. It seems, then, we have so much to say about our *dead* Christ, his miracles and prophecies, that we have but little time to consider our present scourged and forsaken Christ, who stands before us in the human world of to-day, with the thorn-crown piercing its brow! Let us not excuse ourselves, but vail our faces! There is no excuse for our church. We are founded only on the grandeur of human nature, on which also we and our leaders have ever claimed that the mission of the Son of God was founded. With our views of worship there would be no need for a visible, external church, were it not for our mission to humanity. Were there no practical duties toward mankind, our faith would say, "Close the churches, and turn each man all the more on his own soul, so that he may worship not in any outward temple, but in his closet, in spirit and in truth!" Our visible church is a seal to our mission to humanity, as the body is the seal of a soul's mission to other bodies. We stand here for the dignity of man, for his elevation, for every human claim; or else we stand as a wart or a wen on the body. We have a God identified with man; a Bible which says, "If ye love not your brother whom you have seen, how can ye love God whom ye have not seen?"

Our reverence for man does not mean that we are contented with him. No student of history and society can be contented with man, *on account* of this reverence for him. King David, looking up to the splendor of the heavenly host, may ask sadly enough, What is man? He does indeed seem a dwarf in his magnificent palace.

These mountains, oceans, continents *do* suggest a much grander race to rule over them. Yet have we had a few colossal souls,—human continents and mountains. We tread on a planet where Moses, and Plato, and Paul, and Shakspere, and Columbus have stood. That we speak such names with reverence and pride; that we count it noble to belong to the same race, and speak the language of such men—this is the token of an ascending race. Let the scoffer point to war, rapine, cannibalism, to prove the meanness of man: we ask him how do we know that war, rapine, lust, crime, *are* mean? In animals such things are not mean. If we were nothing better, we would not feel that our history, as a race, is disgraceful. Toad is not loathsome to toad, nor viper to viper. Furthermore we ask, Who are our heroes, our loved and admired men? Are they the assassins, the thieves, the more eminent cannibals and murderers? On the walls of the lowliest you shall find portraits of Christ and St. John, of Luther, Wesley, Washington, Chatham, and Wilberforce; not portraits of Caligula, of Judas, or Benedict Arnold.

All around us we see man contending with Destiny in a million forms,—with the earth's barrenness, with temptation and passion, with ignorance and pain; yet ever as we cry out to our watchmen, "What of the night?" the watchmen cry, "The morning cometh!" Then with infinite hope for man, and reverence for his nature, we will look from our Pisgah of Faith for the promised land of humanity; where angels shall at last welcome man with the song, "Thou hast made him a little lower than the angels, and hast crowned him with glory and honor."

www.ingramcontent.com/pod-product-compliance
Lightning Source LLC
LaVergne TN
LVHW020241110826
845151LV00003B/994
* 9 7 8 1 4 2 5 5 2 9 4 1 3 *